T0107599

PREHISTORIC AEGEAN AND NEAR EASTERN METAL TYPES

Søren Dietz, Thanasis J. Papadopoulos and Litsa Kontorli-Papadopoulou

THE NATIONAL MUSEUM OF DENMARK
COLLECTION OF CLASSICAL AND NEAR EASTERN ANTIQUITIES

PREHISTORIC AEGEAN AND NEAR EASTERN METAL TYPES.
Søren Dietz, Thanasis J. Papadopoulos and Litsa Kontorli-Papadopoulou.
THE NATIONAL MUSEUM OF DENMARK COLLECTION OF CLASSICAL
AND NEAR EASTERN ANTIQUITIES.
© The National Museum of Denmark and the authors 2015

Design: Nora Petersen and Søren Dietz
Cover illustration: Copperplate engraving produced by Magnus Petersen for the
unpublished and unfinished manuscript of Christian Blinkenberg concerning
the Prehistoric Aegean Bronzes of the National Museum.

Printed by Narayana Press, Denmark

ISBN: 978 87 7124 938 5

Distributed by AARHUS UNIVERSITY PRESS
www.unipress.dk

The publication was sponsored by Institute for Aegean Prehistory.
2133 Arch Street, Suite 300. Philadelphia. PA 109103. USA (INSTAP)

PREHISTORIC AEGEAN AND NEAR EASTERN METAL TYPES
Søren Dietz, Thanasis J. Papadopoulos and Litsa Kontorli-Papadopoulou

CONTENTS

INTRODUCTION

The present publication attempts to make the collection of Prehistoric Aegean and Near Eastern bronzes in the National Museum of Denmark known to scholars in the field. The late Professor Christian Blinkenberg actually planned a full publication of the Prehistoric Aegean and Italian bronzes, but the manuscript was unfinished at his death in 1948. The steel engravings (frontpage) now kept in the National Museum in Copenhagen were produced for this project.

The catalogue contains all Aegean metals kept in the Department of Ancient Cultures of Denmark and the Mediterranean. In the section on the Near Eastern metals, bronzes from Hama, however, are not included. Except for that, all metal objects from the Near East dated before 1000 BC are found in the catalogue.

Some of the Rhodian metals have been acquired through excavation; the remaining examples have been purchased for, or, in a few instances, presented to the Museum by local authorities. A brief account of the circumstances of acquisition should enable the reader to compare the piece in question with similar material in other museums and to estimate the reliability of the provenances stated in the catalogue.

The first two Prehistoric Aegean bronzes were offered to the Royal Collection by Christian Tuxen Falbe, who bought them in Athens, where he served as Danish Consul General from 1833 to 1835. The arm ring no. 80 was "bought from Athens", while the dagger no. 12 was acquired on Seriphos, with other items from the island. This provenance should thus be considered safe. Both were probably bought in 1834 or not later than 1835. One single arm ring, catalogue no. 81, was bought from Professor Heldreich in Athens in March 1870. The next and much larger acquisition derives from Professor A.S. Rhousopoulos in Athens. The items are mentioned in a letter from Rhousopoulos in November 2, 1872 to J.J.A. Worsaae, who evidently knew about the bronzes beforehand. The provenances are stated by Rhousopoulos (As for the bronzes from the so-called Kythnos/ or Naxos hoard (catalogue nos. 55, 63, 64 and 67), see also a note in the Register in the British Museum from 1866 which reads, "Professor Rhousopoulos says that nos. 1-8 were found together with others in a cave at a considerable distance from the town of Naxos. Others of the find are at Copenhagen" (Lesley Fitton J. in AJA 93, 1989, pp. 31-39). The pieces arrived at the British Museum in 1864, and were finally purchased in 1866. Rhousopoulos probably refers to nos. 3153, 3143 and 3144. The bronzes in the National Museum were actually bought by Mr. Richard Christensen in Athens in 1873 (In addition to finds from Greece, this collection also contained pieces from Magna Graecia).

The sword no. 1 was purchased in Paris in April 1879, from the dealer Fenardent, who in a letter stated that it was found in Amorgos where it was once bought by the archaeologist Rayet (The same year the brewer Carl Jacobsen bought the famous Archaic Rayet head now kept in the Ny Carlsberg Glyptotek, Copenhagen). Later the same year, in November 1879, the three double axes, nos. 48, 51 and 52 and the axe-adze no. 60 were bought from Professor Heldreich in Athens. In addition the same Heldreich delivered three groups of bronzes in 1880: catalogue no. 62 in April, 24, 33, 34 and 35 in May – 71 and 82 in October. Moreover the double axe no. 46 was purchased in Athens in 1880. During a visit to Athens in July 1881, Dr. Sophus Müller, bought the following 11 items – from whom is unfortunately not stated in the files – catalogue nos. 25, 26, 30, 31, 53, 56, 57, 58, 59, 61 and 65. Again in 1887 Sophus Müller visited Athens together with the brewer, Carl Jacobsen. Müller bought the sword, catalogue no. 3 from Rhousopoulos in Athens and the awl no. 85 from Palaeologos. Likewise from Palaeologos, Müller bought the grave group from Arkesine in Amorgos (containing one dagger, catalogue no. 22, and some very significant pottery (Bossert 1954)).

Two bronzes (nos. 45 and 68) with a silver arm ring (no. 84), some pottery and marble objects were purchased by Christian Blinkenberg from Palaeologos in Athens in the spring of 1896. All objects were stated to be from Amorgos (Safe provenances according to Blinkenberg, since Palaeologos owned a house on the island where he spent every summer. The Cycladic marble figurines (4696-4699) from the National Museum are published in extenso in Riis et al. 1989. As for the pottery: inventory nos. 4700-4703 (found 1893), see Blinkenberg and Friis Johansen, Pl. 37, 1-3. The remaining numbers are cores of obsidian: 4681-4686 and various bowls of marble: 4687-4694 (Guides 1995, 11 – in the inventory said to be from graves excavated by Chr. Tsountas. On the trade with antiquities from Amorgos in the late 19th century see Galanakis 2013). In 1904 Blinkenberg bought a series of gold and bone items, flint and obsidian from the dealer Drakopoulos in Athens who stated that the items were bought from the heirs of a peasant who had worked for Schliemann. The objects may have come from Grave Circle A in Mycenae. As this material has never been published before, it has been added as Appendix 1. The flint and obsidian objects were drawn and studied by Mr. Lasse Sørensen of Copenhagen.

In 1912 the National Museum received as a gift from the Museum in Heraklion, among many other items, two objects in bronze: catalogue nos. 23 and 54. All objects had been excavated in Crete, no. 54 was said to be from Selakanos. A fragment of a sword, catalogue no. 7 was found by Blinkenberg in the "Ossuaire Mycenien" on Delos in 1920.

As for the three catalogue numbers with provenance Troy, two were bought by the later Director of the National Museum, Sophus Müller from the dealer Rousopoulos in Athens, 1887 while catalogue number 91 derives from Heinrich Schliemann's excavations at Troy, presented to the National Museum by the excavator himself in 1885. The small collection of Cypriot bronzes had mainly been purchased in Paris in the late 19th century, but some, with safe provenance, are gifts from the Swedish Cyprus expedition and Professor Ejnar Gjerstad in 1935. Finally, as for the Near Eastern bronzes of the collection, a considerable number of these were acquired due to the antiquarian interests of Julius Løytved who served as a Danish Consul in Beirut from 1886 to 1897. The first acquisition (no. 105) was part of a total number of 280 "ancient objects" bought from Løytved in 1878. Later acquisitions are from 1880/1881 (nos. 109, 117 and 118), 1882 (nos. 119, 120 and 121), 1889/1890 (nos. 111 and 115) and finally one bronze object (no. 122 was deposited at the Museum after the death of Løytved in 1912. The bronze dagger with provenance Selemieh (catalogue no. 108) was a gift from one of the members of the expedition to Hama in Syria 1931 to 1938. Some of the Near Eastern bronzes in this catalogue are perhaps not strictly speaking prehistoric in the usual Near Eastern terminology but rather Protohistoric or early Historic.

ACKNOWLEDGEMENTS: The authors are much obliged to the following colleagues and friends: Professor Bernhard Hänsel, Berlin. Professor Hans-Günther Buchholz, Langgänz. Mr. John Lund, senior scholar and Mrs. Bodil Bundgaard Rasmussen, Keeper of the Collection of Near Eastern and Mediterranean Antiquities at the National Museum of Denmark. Drawings were made by Jette Eeg and Poul Wölck. The authors are obliged to Consul General Gösta Enboms Foundation who generously took care of part of the drawing expenses and preparation of the manuscript.

ABBREVIATIONS (except for abbreviations found in AJA Instruction for contributors)

Ancient Cypriot Art 2001: Ancient Cypriot Art in Copenhagen 2001.

ESA X: Przeworski Stefan, "Altorientalische Altertümer in skandinavischen Sammlungen". Eurasia Septentrionalis Antiqua X 1936, 73-128.

GUIDES 1995: Guides to the National Museum. The Collection of Near Eastern and Classical Antiquities. Greeks, Etruscans, Romans. Cph. 1995, 15 (Bodil Bundgaard Rasmussen ed.).

LINDOS IV, 1: Dietz S. Excavations and Surveys in Southern Rhodes: The Mycenaean Period. Publications of the National Museum. Archaeological Historical Series Vol. XXII: 1. Odense 1984.

SCE: Swedish Cyprus Expedition.

Worsaae 1879: Worsaae J.J.A.: "Fra Steen-og Bronzealderen i den gamle og den nye Verden". Aarbøger for nordisk Oldkyndighed og Historie 1879, 249-357.

BIBLIOGRAPHY

Alexiou S. & Warren P. 2004
The Early Minoan Tombs of Lebena Southern Crete. SIMA XXX.

Alram-Stern E. & S. Deger-Jalkotzy 2006
Aigeira I. Die mykenische Akropolis. Faszikel 3. Wien.

Andronikos M. 1969
Βεργίνα I. Τό Νεκροταφείον των Τύμβων. Athens.

Avila R.A.J. 1983
Bronzene Lanzen-und Pfeilspitzen der griechischen Spätbronzezeit. PBFV,1. München.

Barber R.L.N. 1987
The Cyclades in the Bronze Age. London.

Barnett R.D. 1936
"An unrecognized Anatolian Ivory". BMQ X, 121-123.

Barnett R.D. 1975
A Catalogue of the Nimrud Ivories. 2nd ed. Bradford and London.

Benzi M. 1992
Rodi e la Civiltà Mycenea. I-II. Roma.

Benzi M. 1997
"The Late Early Bronze Age Finds from Vathy Cave (Kalymnos) and their links with the Northeast Aegean". In Doumas Ch. G. and V. La Rosa (eds.): Poliochni e l'Antica etá del Bronze Nell'Egeo Settentrionale, 383-394. Athens.

Benzi M. 2005
"A group of Mycenaean Vases and Bronzes from Pyli, Kos". In ΑΕΙΜΝΗΣΤΟΣ. Miscellanea di Studi per Mario Cristofani, Tome I, 15-24. Firenze.

Blinkenberg Chr. 1896
"Præmykenske Oldsager. Bidrag til studiet af Grækenlands ældste Kultur". Aarbøger for Nordisk Oldkyndighed og Historie, 1-64.

Blinkenberg Chr. 1897
"Antiquities prémyceniennes". Memoires de la Societé Royale des Antiquaires du Nord (1896), 1-69.

Blinkenberg Chr. 1926
Fibules grecques et orientales. Lindiaka V. Det Kgl. Danske videnskabernes Selskab, historisk-filologiske Meddelelser, XIII,1. Copenhague.

Blinkenberg Chr. & Friis Johansen K.
CVA Danemark Copenhague: Musée National (no. 1).

Boardman J. 1961
The Cretan Collection in Oxford. The Dictaean Cave and the Iron Age Crete. Oxford.

Palmer L. & Boardman J. 1964
"The Knossos Tablets". Antiquity 38, 45-51.

Bossert H. Th. 1942
Alt-Anatolien. Kunst and Handwerk in Kleinasien von Anfängen bis zum volligen Aufgehen in der griechichen Kultur. Berlin.

Bossert E.-M. 1954
"Zur Datierung der Gräber von Arkesine auf Amorgos". Festschrift P. Goesslar, 23-34.

Bossert E.-M. 1965
Ein Beitrag zu den frühkykladischen Fundgruppen". In Anadolou Arastirmalari. Festschrift Helmuth Th. Bossert. Istanbul. 85-100.

Bouzek J. 1985
The Aegean, Anatolia and Europe: Cultural late relations in the second Millenium B.C. SIMA XXIX. Göteborg.

Braidwood R.J. 1940
"Report on two Sondages on the Coast of Syria, South of Tartous". Syria 21, 183-226.

Braidwood R.J. 1960
Excavations in the Plain of Antioch I. Chicago.

Branigan K. 1966
"Byblite Daggers in Cyprus and Crete". AJA 70,123-126.

Branigan K. 1968
"A Transitional Phase in Minoan Metallurgy". BSA 63, 185-203.

Branigan K. 1969
"Early Aegean Hoards of Metalwork". BSA 64, 1-11.

Branigan 1974
Aegean Metalworks of the Early and Middle Bronze Age. Oxford.

Branigan K. 1977
"Metal Objects and Metal Technology of the Cycladic Culture". In Thimme J. (ed.) Art and culture of the Cyclades. Karlsruhe.

Breitenstein N. 1951
Antik-Cabinettet 1851. Udgivet i Hundredaaret af Nationalmuseet. Copenhagen.

Buchholz H.-G. 1954
"Zur Herkunft der kyprischen Silbenschrift". Minos III, 2, 133-151.

Buchholz H.-G. 1959
Zur Herkunft der kretischen Dobbeltaxt: Geschichte und auswärtige Beziehungen einer minoischen Kult-symbols. Kiel.

Buchholz H.-G. 1960
"Die Doppeltaxt – eine Leitform auswärtiger Beziehungen des ägäischen Kulturkreises". PZ 38, 39-71.

Buchholz H.-G. 1962
"Der Pfeilglätter aus dem VI. Schachtgrab von Mykene und die helladischen Pfeilspitzen". JdI 77, p. 1-58.

Buchholz H.-G. 1983
"Doppeläxte und die Frage der Balkanbeziehungen des ägäischen Kulturkreises". In Ancient Bulgaria. Papers presented to the International Symposium on the Ancient History and Archaeology of Bulgaria. University of Nottingham, 1981. Part I U (1983). Nottingham, 43-134.

Buchholz H.-G. 1987
Alaschia-Zypern (Literaturbericht) in Buchhoz H.(ed.): Ägäische Bronzezeit, Darmstadt, 227-236.

Buchholz H.-G. 1999
Ugarit, Zypern und Ägäis. Kulturbeziehungen im zweiten Jahrtausend v. Chr. Münster.

Buchholz H.-G., Jöhrens G. & Maull J. 1973
"Jagd und Fischfang". Archaeologia Homerica I, J. Göttingen.

Buchholz H.G., Foltiny S. & Höckmann O. 1980
"Kriegswesen. Teil 2. Angriffswaffen". Arch. Homerica I, E, 2. Göttingen.

Buchholz H.-G. & Karageorghis V. 1971
Altägäis und Altkypros. Tübingen.

Buhl M.-L. 1977
"Some Western-Asiatic Bronze Figurines. And a Few Remarks on Julius Løytved as an Antiquarian". ActaArch 48, 139-154.

Caskey J.L. 1957
"Excavations at Lerna 1956". Hesperia 26, 142-162.

Catling H.W. 1956
"Bronze Cut-and –Thrust Swords in the Eastern Mediterranean". PPS XXII, 102-125.

Catling H.W. 1961
"A New Bronze Sword from Cyprus". Antiquity 35, 115-122.

Catling H.W. 1964
Cypriot Bronzework in the Mycenaean World. Oxford.

Catling H.W. 1968
"Late Minoan Vases and Bronzes in Oxford". BSA 63, 89-131.

Caubet A., A. Hermary & V. Karageorghis 1992
Art Antique de Cypre au Musée du Louvre du Chalcolithique à L'Epoque Romaine. Paris.

Chantre E. 1874
L'Age de la pierre et l'age du Bronze en Troade et en Grèce. Lyon.

Collon D. 1972
"The Smiting God. A Study of a Bronze in the Pomerance Collection in New York". Levant 4, 111-134.

Comstock M. & Vermeule C. 1971
Greek, Etruscan & Roman Bronzes in the Museum of Fine Arts Boston. Boston Mass.

Coussin P. 1928
"Sur quelques armes antiques". RA 5. serie, Tome XXVII, 254-277.

Cowen J-D. 1956
"Eine Einführung in die Geschichte der bronzenen Griffzungenschwerter in Süddeutchland und den angrenzenden Gebieten". BRGK 36, 52-155.

Demakopoulou K. 1969
"A Mycenaean bronze sword from Accadia". AAA 2, 226-8.

Despini G. 1979
"Ανασκαφή Τήνου". Prakt, 228-235.

Deshayes J. 1960
Les outils de bronze de l'Indus au Danube (IVe au IIe millénaire). Paris.

Dickinson O.T.P.K. 1977
The Origins of the Mycenaean Civilization. Göteborg.

Dickinson, O. 1994
The Aegean Bronze Age. Cambridge.

Dietz S. 1971
"Aegean and Near-Eastern Metal Daggers in Early and Middle Bronze Age Greece. The Dating of the Byblite hoards and Aegean Imports". ActaArch XLII, 1-22.

Dietz S. & Trolle S. 1974
Arkæologens Rhodos. Copenhagen.

Dietz S. 1980
Asine II. Results of the Excavations East of the Acropolis 1970-1974. Fasc. 2: The Middle Helladic Cemetery and the Early Mycenaean Deposits. Sthlm.

Dietz S. 1991
The Argolid at the Transition to the Mycenaean Age. Studies in the Chronology and Cultural Development in the Shaft Grave Period. Copenhagen.

Druart C. 2006
Analyse Techno – Morphologique et functionnelle des pointes de fleche en Pierre Mycéniennes. (Unpublished master thesis. Université Paris I. Panthéon-Sorbonne). Paris.

Duemmler F. 1886
"Mitteilungen von den griechischen Inseln". AM 11, 15-46.

Duemmler F. 1901
Kleine Schriften 3, Archaeologische Aufsaetze. Leipzig.

Dunand M. 1937
Fouilles de Byblos 1926-1932. Tome I, Atlas. Paris.

Dunand M. 1939
Fouilles de Byblos, 1926-1932 I, Atlas. Paris.

Dunand M. 1950
Fouilles de Byblos, 1933-1938. Tome II, Atlas. Paris.

Dunand M. 1954
Fouilles de Byblos, 1933-1938. Tome II, Texte pt. 1. Paris.

Dunand M. 1958
Fouilles de Byblos, 1933-1938. Tome II, Texte pt. 2. Paris.

Dörpfeld W. 1927
Alt-Ithaka. München.

Ellis 1968
Foundation Deposits in Ancient Mesopotamia. Massachusetts.

Evely R. D. G. 1993
Minoan crafts: Tools and Techniques – an introduction (SIMA XCII:1). Göteborg.

Fischer A., Vemming Hansen P. & Rasmussen P. 1984
"Macro and Micro Wear Traces on Lithic Projectile Points. Experimental Results and Prehistoric Examples". Journal of Danish Archaeology vol. 3, 19-46.

Fitton J. Lesley 1989
"Esse Quam Videre: A Reconsideration of the Kythnos Hoard of Early Cycladic Tools". AJA 93, 31-39.

Flinders Petrie W.M. 1917
Tools and Weapons. British School of Archaeology in Egypt and Egyptian Research Account 22 year 1916. London.

Flinders Petrie W.M 1925.
Tombs of the Courtiers and Oxyrhynkhos. British School of Archaeology in Egypt, and E.R.A. (Egyptian Research Account) 28th year, 1922. London.

Galanakis Y. 2013
"Early Prehistoric Research in Amorgos and the beginning of Cycladic Archaeology". AJA 117, 2. 181-205.

Giannopoulos Th.G. 2008
Die letzte Elite der mykenischen Welt. Achaia in mykenischer Zeit und das Phänomen der Krieger-bestatuttungen in 12.-11 Jahrhundert v.Chr. Bonn, 168-178.

Goldman H. 1931
Excavations in Eutresis in Boeotia. Cambridge Mass.

Grammenou D.B. & Tzaxili I. 1994.
"Ο Θησαυρός των Πετραλώνων της Χαλκιδικής". ArchEphem, 75-116.

Hamilakis Y. 2003
"The scared geography of hunting: Wild animals, social power and gender in early farming societies". In: Zooarchaeology in Greece. E. Kotjabopoulou, Y. Hamilakis, P. Halstead, C. Gamble & P. Elefanti (eds.). BSA studies 10, 239-248. London.

Harding A. 1975
"Mycenaean Greece and Europe: the evidence of Bronze Tools". PPS 41, 183-202.

Harding A. 1984
The Mycenaeans in Europe. London.

Harding A. 1995
Die Schwerter im ehemaligen Jugoslawien. PBF IV, 14. Stuttgart.

Helbig W. 1909
"Ein homerishces Rundschield mit einem Bügel" JOEAI XII, 1-70.

Hestrin R. & Tadmor M. 1963
"A Hoard of Tools and Weapons from Kfar Monash". IEJ 13, 265-288.

Higgins R.A. 1967
Minoan and Mycenaean Art. London.

Höckmann O. 1980
"Lanze und Speer im spätminoischen und mykenischen Griechenland". JRGZM 27, 13-158.

Höckmann O. 1987
"Lanzen und Speere der ägäischen Bronzezeit und des Übergangs zur Eisenzeit". In Buchholz: Ägäische Bronzezeit. Darmstadt, 329-358.

Iakovidis S. 1969/1970
Περατή. Το Νεκροταφείον. Vols. I-III. Athens.

Inizan M. L., M. Reduron-Ballinger, H. Roche & J. Tixier 1999.
"Technology and terminology of knapped stone". Préhistoire de la Pierre Taillée, 5, Nanterre.

Jacobi G. 1933
"Nuovi scavi nella necropoli micenaea di Ialisso". ASAtene 13-14, 1930-1931, Bergamo, 253-345.

Kardulias P. N. 1999
"Flaked stone and the Role of the Palaces in the Mycenaean World system". In: Rethinking Mycenaean
Palaces: New Interpretations of an Old Idea. Parkinson W. & M. Galaty (eds.). Los Angeles. 61-71.

Karo G. 1930-33
Die Schachtgräber von Mykenai. München.

Kilian K. 1976
"Nordgrenze der ägäischen Kulturbereiches in mykenischer und nachmykenischer Zeit". Jahresbericht des
Instituts für Vorgeschichte der Universität Frankfurt A.M., 112-129.

Kilian K. 1986
"Il confine settentrionale della Civilta' Micenea nella tarda eta' del Bronzo". In: Traffici Micenei nel
Mediterraneo. Problemi storici e documentazione archeologica. Taranto, 283-293.

Kilian-Dirlmeier I. 1993
Die Schwerter in Griechenland (außerhalb der Peloponnes), Bulgarien und Albanien. Prähistorische
Bronzefunde IV,12. Stuttgart.

Kilian-Dirlmeier I. 1997
Das Mittelhelladische Schachtgrab von Ägina.

Kontorli-Papadopoulou L. 2003
"Late Mycenaean Achaean Vases and Bronzes in Berlin". AM 118, 23-47.

Laffineur R. 1974
"L'incrustation à l'époque Mycénienne". L'Antiquité Classique XLIII. Bruxelles, 5-37.

Lamb W. 1929
Greek and Roman Bronzes. London.

Lambrou-Phillipson C. 1990
Hellenorientalia. Near- Eastern Presence in the Bronze Age Aegean, ca. 3000-1100 BC. Göteborg.

Loud G. 1948
Megiddo II. Chicago.

Luce J.V. 1969
The end of Atlantis. London and New York.

Maiuri A. 1926
"Ialysos, scavi della Missione Archeologica Italiana a Rodi". ASAtene VI-VII, 83-256. Bergamo.

Mallowan M. E.L. 1948
"A copper rein-ring from Southern Iraq". Iraq X, 51-55, Pls. VII-VIII.

Maran J. 2001
"Der Depotfund von Petralona (Nordgriechenland) und der Symbolgehalt von Waffen in der ersten Hälfte des 3. Jahrtausends v. Chr. zwischen Karpatenbecken und Ägäis. Lux Orientis". Archäologie zwischen Asien und Europa. Festschrift für Harald Hauptmann zum 65. Geburtstag. Rahden, 275-284.

Matthäus H. 1979
"Two Mycenaean Bronzes" BSA 74, 163 – 173.

Mee Chr. 1982
Rhodes in the Bronze Age. Warminster.

Milojcic V. 1955
"Einige mitteleuropäische Fremdlinge auf Kreta", JRGZM 2, 153-169.

Montelius O. 1900
Die Chronologie der ältesten Bronzezeit in Norddeutschland und Skandinavien. Braunschweig.

Montelius O. 1924
La Grèce Préclassique I. Sthlm.

Montet P. 1928
Byblos et L'Égypte. Paris.
Morricone L. 1967
"Eleonae e Langada: Sepolcreti della tarda Età del Bronzo a Coo". ASAtene NS 27-28, 5-611.

Morricone L. 1975
"Coo-Scavi e scoperte nel Serraglio e in località minori (1935-43)". ASAtene L-LI (NS XXXIV-XXXV, 1972-73), 139-396.

Mortensen P. 1962
"To mykenske Pragtsværd". Nationalmuseets Arbejdsmark 1962. Copenhagen, 120-122.

Moschos I. 2002
"Western Achaea during the LHIIIC period. Approaching the latest excavation evidence. In Gli Achei e l'Identità Etnica degli Achei d'Occidente". Atti del Convegne Internazionale di Studi. Paestum, 23-25 febbraio 2001, Fondazione Paestum Tekmeria 3, Paestum-Atene, 15-40.

Müller S. 1882
"Den europæiske Bronzealders Oprindelse og første Udvikling, oplyst ved de ældste Bronzefund I det sydøstlige Europa" Aarbøger for Nordisk Arkæologi og Historie, 279-356.

Müller S. 1884
"Ursprung und erste Entwicklung der europäischen Bronzekultur beleuchtet durch die ältesten Bronzefunde im südöstlichen Europa. Entwurf zu einer archäologischen Untersuchung". Archiv für Anthropologie XV. Band. Braunschweig, 323-355.

Møller-Christensen V. 1938
The History of the Forceps. Kbh.-Lond.

Naue J. 1903
Die vorrömischen Schwerter aus Kupfer, Bronze ind Eisen. München.

Negbi O. 1961
"On two Bronze figurines with Plumed Helmets from the Louvre Collection." IEJ 11, 111-117.

Negbi O. 1968
"Dating some groups of Canaanite bronze figurines". PEQ 100, 45-55.

Negbi O. 1976
"Canaanite Goods in Metal. An Archaeological Study of Ancient Syro-Palestinian Figurines". Tell Aviv University-Institute of Archaeology. Tell Aviv.

Page D.L. 1970
The Santorini Eruption and the Destruction of Minoan Crete. London.

Papathanathopoulos G. 1961/62
"Κυκλαδικά Νάξου". ArchDelt 17, A, 104-151.

Papadopoulos Th.J. 1979
Mycenaean Achaea. SIMA LV. Göteborg.

Papadopoulos Th. J. 1987
"Zum Stand der Bronzezeitforschung in Epiros". In: Buchholz H.-G. (ed.): Ägäische Bronzezeit. Darmstadt, 359-377.

Papadopoulos Th.J. 1998
The Late Bronze Age Daggers of the Aegean I. The Greek Mainland. Prähistorische Bronzefunde. Abt. VI. Band 11. Stuttgart.

Papadopoulos Th. J. 1999
"Warrior-graves in Achaean Mycenaean Cemeteries". In: Polemos. Le Contexte Guerrier en Égée à âge du Bronze. Aegaeum 19, Liege, 267-273.

Papadopoulos Th. & Kontorli-Papadopoulos L. 1984
"Notes from Achaea". BSA 79, 221-227.

Papadopoulos Th. & Kontorli-Papadopoulou L. 2000
"Four Late Bronze Age Italian Imports in Achaea", in PERIPLUS. Feschtrift für Hans-Günter Buchholz zu seinem achtzigsten Geburtstag am 24. December 1999, SIMA CXXVII, Jonsered, 143-146, pls. 35-36.

Papadopoulos Th. & Kontorli-Papadopoulou L. 2001
"Death, Power and Troubles in Late Mycenaean Peloponnese, the évidence of Warrior Graves", in Contributions to the Archaeology and History of the Bronze and Iron Ages in the Eastern Mediterranean. Studies in Honour of Paul Äström" (ed. P.Fischer),Wien, 127-138.

Papadopoulos Th. & Kontorli-Papadopoulou L. 2003
"Προϊστορική Αρχαιολογία Δυτικής Ελλάδας Ιόνιων Νησιών". Ioannnina.

Papadopoulos TH. & Kontorli-Papadopoulou l. 2009
Power, Troubles and Death in Late Bronze Aegean and Cyprus: the evidence of warrior-graves and painting", Athanasia. The Earthy, the Celestial and the Underworld in the Mediterranean from the Late Bronze and the Early Iron Age. International Archaeological Conference, Rhodes 2009 (ed. N. Stambo;idis-) Herakleio, 239-248.

Papazoglou-Manioudaki L. 1994
"A Mycenaean warrior's tomb at Krini near Patras". BSA 89, 172-200.

Papazoglou-Manioudaki L. 1999
"Πήλινα και Χάλκινα της Πρώιμης Μυκηναϊκής εποχής απο τήν Αχαια". Α' Διεθνές Διεπιστημονικό Συμπόσιο, Η Περιφέρεια του Μυκηναϊκού Κόσμου (1994). Lamia, 269-283.

Parkinson W.A. 1999
"Chipping away at a Mycenaean Economy. Obsidian Exchange, Linear B and Palatial Control in Late Bronze Age Messenia". In: Rethinking Mycenaean Palaces: New Interpretations of an Old Idea. Parkinson W. & M.Galaty (eds.). Los Angeles, 73-85.

Parrot A., Chéhab M.H. & Moscati S. 1975
Les Phéniciens. Berlin.

Perrot G. 1886
"Note sur quelques poignards de Mycènes". BCH X, 341-356.

Petropoulos M. 1995
"Νικολέϊκα Αίγίου, Καλλιθέα μυκηναϊκό νεκροταφείο". ArchDelt 50, 233-236.

Petropoulos M. 2006
"Ρακίτα – Νικολέικα – Ελίκη – Σαλμενίκο". 'Αρχαιολογική Σύνοδος Νότιας και Δυτικής Ελλάδος, Πάτρα 9-12 Ιουνίου 1996. Πρακτικά. Athens.

Porada E. 1942
"The Warrior with Plumed Helmet. A Study of Syro-Cappadocian Cylinder Seals and Bronze Figurines". Berytus VII, 57-63.

Prendi F. 2002
"Les relations entre L'Albanie et L'Égée à travers la préhistoire". In: Touchais G. et J. Renard: L'Albanie dans L'Europe Préhistorique. BCH supplement 42, 85-96.

Przeworski S. 1939
Die Metallindustrie Anatoliens in der Zeit von 1500-700 vor Chr. Zeitschrift (?) Inst. Arch. F. Ethnographie (?) Bd. XXXVI, Suppl. Tf. XVIII, 1.

Randsborg K. 1967
"Aegean Bronzes in a Grave from Jutland". Acta Arch. 38, 1-27.

Rashid Subhi Anwar 1983
Gründungsfiguren in Iraq. Prähistorische Bronzefunde I, 2. München.

Renfrew C. 1967
"Cycladic Metallurgy and the Aegean Early Bronze Age". AJA 71, 1-20.

Renfrew 1972
The Emergence of Civilization. The Cyclades and the Aegean in the Third Millenium B.C. London.

Richter G.M.A. 1915
The Metropolitan Museum of Art. Greek, Etruscan and Roman Bronzes. New York.

Riis P.J. 1957
Fortidens Kultur I, 27.

Saidah R. 1993-1994
"Beirut in the Bronze Age: The Kharji Tombs". Berytus 41, 137-210.

Salonen A.
Die Wasserfahrzeuge in Babylonien. Helsinki.

Sandars N.K. 1955
"The Antiquity of the One-edged Bronze Knife in the Aegean". PPS 20, 174-197.

Sandars N.K. 1958-1959
"A Minoan Cemetery on Upper Gypsades. The Bronzes". BSA 53-54, 232-237.

Sandars N.K. 1961
"The First Aegean Swords and their Ancestry". AJA 65, 17-29.

Sandars N.K. 1963
"Later Aegean Bronze Swords". AJA 67, 118-153.

Sandars N.K. 1978
The Sea Peoples, Warriors of the Ancient Mediterranean 1250-1150, London.

Sarzec E. de & L. Heuzey 1884-1912
Découvertes en Chaldée, Vol. I-III.

Schaeffer C.F.A. 1936
"Les fouilles de Ras Shamra-Ugarit. Septième Campagne (Printemps 1935)." Syria XVII, 105-148.

Schaeffer C.F.A. 1948
Stratigraphie Comparée et Chronologie de l'Asie Occidentale (IIIe et IIe millénaires). London.

Schaeffer C.F.A. 1949
Ugaritica II. Paris.

Schliemann H. 1878
Mykenae: Bericht über meine Forschungen und Entdeckungen in Mykenae und Tiryns. Darmstadt.

Schliemann H. 1880
The City and Country of the Trojans. London.

Schliemann H. 1886
Tiryns: Der prähistorische Palast der Könige von Tiryns. Ergebnisse der neuesten Ausgrabungen. Leipzig.

Schmidt H. 1902
Heinrich Schliemann's Sammlung trojanischer Altertümer. Berlin.

Sherratt S. 2000
Catalogue of Cycladic Antiquities in the Ashmolean Museum. The Captive Spirit. Vol. I. Text. Vol II. Illustrations. Oxford.

Snodgrass A. 1967
Arms and Armours of the Greeks. London.

Spyropoulos Th.G. 1972
Υστερομυκηναικοί Ελλαδικοί Θησαυροί. Athens.

Stronach D. 1957
"The development and diffusion of early metal types in Early Bronze Age Anatolia". AnatSt 7, 89-125.

Strøm Ingrid 1982
Grækenlands Forhistoriske Kulturer II. Minoisk og Tidlig Mykensk Kultur. Viborg.

Todorova H. 1981
Die kupferzeitlichen Äxte und Beile in Bulgarien. PBF Abteilung IX, 14. München.

Tsountas Chr. 1898
"Κυκλαδικά". ArchEphem 16, 137-211.

Tsountas Chr. 1899
"Κυκλαδικά II". ArchEphem 17, 74-134.

Tsountas Chr. -Manatt 1897
The Mycenaean Age: A Study of the Monuments and Culture of Pre-Homeric Greece. Boston/New York.

Undset I. 1890
III. Die ältesten Schwertformen. ZfE, 1-29.

Vermeule E. 1964
Greece in the Bronze Age. Chicago.

Vulpe A. 1975
Die Äxte und Beile in Rumänien II. PBF Abteilung IX, 5. München.

Weber H. 1944
"Angriffswaffen". In: Kunze E. & Schleiff H. Olympische Forschungen I, 146-165. Berlin.

White Muscarella O. 1988
Bronze and Iron. Ancient Near Eastern Artifacts in the Metropolitan Museum of Art. New York.

Woolley C.L. 1934
Ur Excavations vol. II (Text and Plates). The Royal Cemetery. Oxford.

Woolley C.L. 1936
"Tal Atchana". JHS LVI, 125-134.

Woolley L. 1955
Alalakh. Oxford.

Worsaae J.J.A. 1881
"Des ages de pierre et de bronze dans l'ancien et le nouveaux monde". Mémoires des la Societé Royale des antiquaries du Nord 1880, 131-244.

Xenaki-Sakellariou A. and Chatziliou Ch. 1989
"Peinture en Metal" a l'epoque Mycenienne. Athenes.

Zachos, K. 2007
"The Neolithic Background: A Reassessment". In P. M. Day and R. C. P. Doonan (eds.) Metallurgy in the Early Bronze Age Aegean, Sheffield Studies in Aegean Archaeology 7: 168-206. Oxford: Oxbow Books.

Zachos K. 2010
"Η μεταλλουργία στην Ελλάδα και στη ΝΑ Ευρώπη κατά την 5η και 4η χιλιετία π.Χ.". In: Papadimitriou N.: Η Ελλάδα στο ευρύτερο πολιτισμικό των Βαλκανίων κατά την 5η και 4η χιλιετία π.Χ. Athens, 77-91.

Zeravica Z. 1993
Äxte und Beile aus Dalmatien und anderen Teilen Kroatiens, Montenegro, Bosnien und Herzegowina. PBF Abteilung IX, 18. Stutgart.

Zettler R.L. and L. Horne (eds.) 1998
Treasures from the Royal Tombs of Ur. Philadelphia.

Åström P. 1977
The Cuirass Tomb and other Finds at Dendra. Part I: The Chamber Tombs (SIMA IV). Göteborg.

CATALOGUE

THE GREEK MAINLAND AND THE AEGEAN ISLANDS
- Swords
- Daggers
- Spearheads
- Knives
- Double-axes
- Socketed axes
- Axe/adze
- Flat axes/chisels
- Arm rings
- Various

TROY

CYPRUS
- Flat axes/chisels
- Daggers
- Spearheads
- Various

THE NEAR EAST
- Swords
- Daggers
- Spearheads
- Knives
- Socketed axes
- Bronze rings
- Bronze figurines
- Bowls
- Various

APPENDIX: A note on some Mycenaean gold objects, obsidian and flint arrowheads bought in 1904 by Christian Blinkenberg from Drakopoulos in Athens. The dealer stated that the objects had been purchased from "the heirs of a peasant who had worked for Schliemann".

ABBREVIATIONS
D: Diameter
L: Length
Th: Thickness
W: Width

THE GREEK MAINLAND AND THE AEGEAN ISLANDS

SWORDS

No. 1 (Inventory no. 3163/O.A. VII b 44). Well-preserved sword blade. Fragments of the edges are missing. Flat blade (0.2 cm thick) with pronounced square midrib. Two circular nail holes (diam. 0.5 cm) at top of the blade.
L 58.8 cm. Max. W 4.0 cm
Provenance: Amorgos. Bought in April 1879 from the antique dealer Fenardent in Paris who, in a letter, states that it was found in Amorgos, "where it was in the past bought by the archaeologist Rayet" (first seen by Sophus Müller in 1878).
Published: Worsaae 1879, 346 and 344, Fig. 16. (ref. Undset 1880, 152, Pl. 18,3). Undset 1890, 14f., Fig. 25. Montelius 1924, 106, Pl. 9, 2. Coussin 1928, 259, Fig. 3. Riis 1957, 27. Kilian-Dirlmeier 1993, 9, no. 1, Tf. 1 ("Griffplattenschwerter")
Comments: DATING: EC/EH II-III according to Kilian–Dirlmeier 1993 (9-10 with further references). DISTRIBUTION: The Cyclades, the Dodecanese (Kos), Leukas (Nidri) (Kilian-Dirlmeier 1993, 10), Bulgaria (Kilian-Dirlmeier 1993, 9).

No. 2 (Inventory no. 3164/O.A. VII b 36). Badly damaged sword blade (in three pieces). Part of tang and point missing. The blade has a pointed, ovoid section. Two thin parallel plastic ribs on each side of the pointed triangular midrib are out-curving at the top of the blade. Flat tang.
L (as preserved) 68.0 cm. W (at tang) 1.2 cm. Max. Th 1.3 cm
Provenance: Amorgos. From Rhousopoulos 1873. R. Christensen, Febr. 1873 (Amorgos (10?)).
Published: Worsaae 1879, 346 and 344, Fig. 12. (ref. Remouchamps in Internationales Archiv für Etnographie XXVIII, 1927, p. XLI, note 5). Montelius 1924, 106, Pl. 9, 1 (incorrectly reconstructed). Branigan 1974, 16, no. 491, Table 11 (incorrectly reconstructed). Kilian-Dirlmeier 1993, 17, no. 17, Tf. 4 (Variant 1).
Comments: Karo Tp. A. For a very similar piece: Branigan 1977, 119 (also in Barber 1987, 101, Fig. 74) and Renfrew 1967 (cat. No. 71), Pl. 5 and Pl. 8 (Class VII). DATING: MMII-LMI/MHIII-LHI/IIA (Kilian-Dirlmeier 1993, 26ff). DISTRIBUTION: East Crete, Peloponnese, Amorgos, N. Epirus and Albania, Rumania (Kilian-Dirlmeier 1993, 28, Tf. 60).

No. 3 (Inventory no. 3249) (see front page no. 3). Well-preserved, horned sword with folded horns. The pronounced midrib with an almost square section (more square than indicated on the drawing, Sandars 1963, Pl. 23,18) has two neatly incised parallel lines on each side. The edges have been sharpened. The corrosion on the one side indicates that the original organic inlay on the hilt had a straight horizontal termination between the lower ends of the folded horns. Straight horizontal termination at the upper part of the hilt.
L 68.1 cm. W (at horns) 6 cm
Provenance: Galaxidi. Bought by Sophus Müller on a journey in April/May 1887 from Rhousopoulos in Athens (who gave the provenance as Galaxidi).
Published: Undset 1890, 14, Fig. 23. Riis 1957, 27. Sandars 1963, 146 and fig. 23, 18. Den Græske Bystat. DR 1980, 4. Kilian-Dirlmeier 1993, 45, no. 62, Tf. 12 ("Hörnerschwerter" Typ 1a).
Comments: Sandars type Cii (Kilian-Dirlmeier 1993, 53). DATING: SM/SHII-SM/SHIIIA DISTRIBUTION: East Crete, Argolid, Phocis, Boiotia, Thessaly, Epirus and the Dodecanese. The distribution is discussed in Kilian-Dirlmeier 1993, 54ff, Tf. 62.

No. 4 (Inventory no. 3166/O.A. VII b 40). Broad tang and upper part of blade of a flange-hilted short sword. The surface is rather badly corroded. The tang shows deep flanges with slightly incurved sides running into angular shoulders, likewise with incurved sides at the upper part of the blade. The incurved upper termination of the tang is the original end of the haft. No nail holes are found in the tang (as can be clearly seen also on the X-ray photo), but remains of bone or ivory inlay are visible between the upraised sides and at the upper part of the blade. This inlay on the blade surrounded a circular area between the square shoulders. Embedded in the inlay material of the tang, seven circular grooves are visible, showing traces of bronze nails on a line (decoration?).

Max. L 12.7 cm. Max. W (tang) 2.1 cm. W at shoulders 6.3 cm. Max Th 1.2 cm. D. of nail prints 0.4 cm
Provenance: Thera. From Rhousopoulos 1873. R. Christensen, February1873 (Thera) (25).
Published: Worsaae 1879, 346 and 344, fig. 13. Montelius 1924, Pl. 9, 8. Kilian-Dirlmeier 1993, 38, no. 50, Tf. 9.
Comments: "Karo Tp. B, close to Variante 3" (Kilian-Dirlmeier 1993, 38). DATING: Probably LHI (see discussion in Kilian-Dirlmeier 1993, 39f). DISTRIBUTION: Peloponnese, Greek Mainland (East), the Dodecanese and Asia Minor (Kilian-Dirlmeier 1993, Tf. 61).

No. 5 (Inventory no. 5668). Well-preserved short sword, the very point of the blade has been glued. The handle has flanged edges to secure the (now lost bone?) inlay. The top of the handle terminates in a narrow, flat, square tang. The shoulders are shaped like short pointed wings. The flat dirk-like blade has three incised lines down the central part.
L 35.7 cm
Provenance: Siana, Rhodes. Bought in Rhodes in 1904 from a dealer who stated that it was found in a Mycenaean grave near Siana in Southern Rhodes (West) together with catalogue numbers 32 and 43.
Published: Sandars 1963, 152, Fig. 27, 53. Dietz & Trolle 1974, 32, Fig. 23. Kilian-Dirlmeier 1993, 49 no. 97, Tf. 18 ("Hörnerschwerter" Typ 2b 1).
Comments: Sandars Class H: "Siana Group Bronzes" (Sandars 1963, 140). DATING: LHIIIB (Kilian-Dirlmeier 1993, 53. Context from Ialysos gr. LIII (Benzi 1992, 173 and 347 ff. Tf. 178)). A dating in IIIA2/early IIIB is suggested by Benzi (Benzi 2005, 17-18, Fig. 13 (a sword from Pyli in Kos). Also Kilian-Dirlmeier 1993, 49, no. 99, Tf. 18)). DISTRIBUTION: The Dodecanese and W. Anatolia (Pergamon).

No. 6 (Inventory no. 12412). Short sword with T-flanged pommel. The grip has raised edges. The sword is almost intact, only lacking a triangular piece of the blade. Below the pommel are two U-shaped concavities which, through two edged beads, run into the grip with parallel sides. The transition to the blade is marked by two square shoulders. There is a horizontal burr across the blade at the lower termination of the shoulder-part. This border marks the lower limit to the extent of the original covering of organic material (bone or ivory). At the side of the grip (where the edges are parallel) and at the top of the pommel is a faint notch (W: 0.5 cm) along the centre line. The three nails in the grip are preserved, the uppermost (placed in the pommel) is broken, however. The blade is slightly in-curved (caused by sharpening?).
L 39.0 cm. W (at pommel) 7.0 cm
Provenance: Passia Grave 2, Rhodes. Gift to the National Museum from the Carlsberg Foundation. Excavated by K.F. Kinch 1904.
Published: Dietz & Trolle 1974, 32, Fig. 22. Lindos IV, 1, 34, Fig. 25. Kilian-Dirlmeier 1993, 83, no. 186, Tf. 29 (Kilian-Dirlmeier Typ F2 (F2A 2).
Comments: Sandars Type F (Sandars 1963, 133 f and 150ff). Catling type Fii (Catling 1968, 95ff). LINDOS IV, 1, 99. DATING: LHIIIA2/LHIIIB/C (Kilian-Dirlmeier 1993, 87). DISTRIBUTION: Greek Mainland, Ionian Islands, the Dodecanese and Crete. Surbo/Lecce, Apulia (Kilian-Dirlmeier 1993, 90ff. and Lindos IV, 99). Syria, Hama (5B 964 Hama F).

No. 7 (Inventory no. 12755). Fragmented, badly corroded piece of a flange hilt. One broken nail hole in the centre.
L (as preserved) 7.2 cm. Max. W 2.4 cm. Nail hole D 0.4 cm
Provenance: Found in the "Ossuaire mycenien" on Delos by Christian Blinkenberg (reference to Fougerés 1891, 494). Found on the surface approximately in the centre of the tholos.
Unpublished
Comments: Probably from a Type B sword (see above catalogue no. 4).

No. 8 (Inventory no. 3165/O.A. VIIb25). The lower part of a blade with a broad pointed oval midrib. Part of the point is missing.
L (as preserved) 25 cm. W 3.4 cm. Th 0.6 cm

Provenance: Corinth. From Rhousopoulos 1873 (who stated the provenance). Not mentioned by R. Christensen.

Published: Worsaae 1879, 344, Fig. 14 and 346. Undset 1890, 16, Fig. 27.

Comments: The blade probably derives from a "Griffzungenschwert"/Naue II sword. See also Harding 1995 passim (for former Yugoslavia). Kilian-Dirlmeier 1993, 94ff. DATING: In the Aegean/Argolid, Late LHIIIB/IIIC (Kilian-Dirlmeier 1993, 100ff). In Achaea, the type is dated to LHIIIC. Papazoglou-Maniodaki (Papazoglou-Manioudaki 1994a, 181) expressed the opinion that "... type II swords were introduced in Achaea during the course of LHIIIC (= Middle/Late IIIC?) while they were already known in the Argolid prior to the collapse of the Mycenaean palatial society". DISTRIBUTION: Discussed by Kilian-Dirlmeier and Harding cit. As for "Naue II" swords from the Peloponnese: Nine "Naue II" swords are reported from Western Achaea: 1) 3 from Kallithea and Kangadhi (Papadopoulos 1979, 166, Figs. 320, a-b, 355, c-d, 356, a-b. Especiallly PMX 292 from Kangadhi is close to our blade) 2) 1 further from Krini, Patras (Papazoglou-Manioudaki 1994a, 177 ff.) 3) 1 from Anthea/Anthaia near Patras (Catling 1956. Discussed and depicted in Papadopoulos and Kontorli-Papadopoulos 1984, 221-224) 4) 2 from Lousiká (Spaliareika) 5) Further 1 from Krini (Monodendri, Agh. Konstantinos) (Papazoglou-Manioudaki 1994a, 180) 6) 1 from Achaia Klauss (Papazoglou-Manioudaki 1994a, 180 and Papadopoulos 1999, 270) 7) 1 from Portes-Kephalovryson (Moschos 2002, 29). In contrast only one "Naue II" sword is reported from Eastern Achaia (Aigion, Nikoleika, Petropoulos 1995, 233-236). Catling (1956, 109 ff.) counts three swords from Mycenae and two from Tiryns (See also Spyropoulos 1972 for the hoards). One "Naue II" sword is reported from Arcadia (Demakopoulou 1969, 226-228 (LHIIIC)). A total of 32 Naue II swords are reported to have been found in Greece, among these 16 are from Achaia (Ioannis Moschos personal information).

No. 9 (Inventory no. 3191/OA VII b 41). Lower part of a sword blade with point. Broad, square midrib and triangular point.

L (as preserved) 11.5 cm. Max. W 3.2 cm

Provenance: Thera (transferred from the Ethnographical Department 1886).

Published: Worsaae 1879, 346 and 344, Fig. 15.

Comments: DATING: LHI (Papadopoulos 1998 (Tp. II, Variant B), 11, 13, Pls. 7: 47, 8: 53 (Mycenae Circle B, grave Γ).

No. 10 (Inventory no. 14417) (Fig. 1). Long bronze sword with gold ornaments. Lower part of the blade is missing. The grip has flanged edges with gold foil preserved on the sides and on the upward-pointing, horned shoulders. Three nails with gold foil are preserved in the grip and two nails below the shoulders at the transition to the blade. The (now lost) covering of the grip is indicated by impressions in the bronze and terminates below the shoulders in an oval opening above the two nails. The oval ivory pommel has a markedly swollen upper side and a concave underside with a grooved square hole where the (not preserved) tang of the handle joined the pommel. Two nails in the pommel were used to fix the tang. The pommel is covered with thin gold strips (L 8.0-5.0 mm, W 0.5 mm, Th 0.2-0.15 mm) fixed in parallel rows mutually displaced to the pommel by pins on the back of the ivory. After hammering a pattern with connected spirals was chased into the gold surface. A similar pattern is seen on one of the flanges.

L (preserved) 30.8 cm. (restored) 43.3 cm. Max. W (at shoulders) 9.3 cm/at grip 2.2 cm. H of pommel: 4.7 cm. W of pommel: 7.6 cm. Th of pommel: 6.7 cm

Provenance: Allegedly from Dendra. Probably from Chamber Tomb 12 in Dendra.

Published: Ars Antiqua, Auktion III, 29, April 1961, Luzerne (Frontispiece and pp. 30f (no. 70)). Mortensen 1962, 120-122. Palmer and Boardman 1963. Randsborg 1967, 26. Åström 1977, 18, nos. 30-31, Pl. VII, 1-2. Strøm 1982, Fig. 425. GUIDES 1995, 15.

Comments: Karo Tp. B (mentioned Sandars 1963, 117 ff.). Also Kilian-Dirlmeier 1993, 5 and 70 (n. 48). "Hörnerschwerter Tp. 1a" (Kilian-Dirlmeier 1993, 43 ff.). Analyses of the metals (Randsborg 1967) indicate that approximately 12% tin has been used for the bronze. The central part was heated and hammered after the casting. DATING: LHIIB/IIIA1 (according to context in Dendra, Chamber tomb 12). DISTRIBUTION: Discussed by Kilian-Dirlmeier 1993, 43 ff.

No. 11 (Inventory no. 14418 (Fig. 1)). Sword with gold ornament. Lower part of the blade is missing or reconstructed. The flanges on the grip are covered in gold foil. A circular nail hole is placed in the middle of the flat grip. Two rounded shoulders likewise covered in gold foil, mark the transition between grip and blade. The now lost bone/ivory of the hilt extended down to the shoulders where two gold plated nails kept the cover of the grip. The blade has a high, flattened midrib. No pommel was recovered.
L 38.3 cm (as reconstructed). W 6.5 cm (at shoulders)
Provenance: Allegedly from Dendra. Probably from Chamber Tomb 12 in Dendra.
Published: Ars Antiqua, Auktion III, 29, April 1961, Luzerne, 30-31, kat. no. 70 (and colour plate). Verdelis in Arch. Chron. 1957, 5-18. Vermeule 1964, Pl. XXI, B. Randsborg 1967, 13, fig. 7c, 10 note 12. Strøm 1982, Fig. 425. GUIDES 1995, 15.
Comments: Sandars Type D1. "Kreuzschwerter Tp. 1b" (Kilian-Dirlmeier 1993, 59, note 6). Ialysos Rhodes (gr. 45) (Benzi 1992, 330 and Tav. 178, b (LH IIIA1). DATING: LHIIB/IIIA1 (according to context in Dendra, Chamber Tomb 12). DISTRIBUTION: Crete (East and West), the Dodecanese, Peloponnese, Attica, Boiotia, Epirus, Thessaly and Albania (Kilian-Dirlmeier 1993. Matthäus 1979, 165, Fig. 3 (Sandars Tp. D1)).

DAGGERS
No. 12 (Inventory no. ABa 341). Dagger with a broad, rather low midrib with an oval section. The top of the blade is flat, with a curving line separating the blade from the haft. Slightly damaged, but preserved in its full length.
L 20.8 cm. Max. W 4.1 cm
Provenance: Serifos. Bought on Serifos by Consul General C.T. Falbe 1844/45.
Published: Compte-rendu du Congrès International d' Anthropologie et d' Archéologie de Copenhague 1869, 482. Breitenstein 1951, 109. Branigan 1974, 161, Cat. No. 315 (8) "Long Daggers Type XIVa".
Comments: DATING: LHIIB/LHIIIA1. The blade is similar to one from Brysari, Achaia. (Papazoglou-Manioudaki 1994b, 276 and Fig. 28). The nails, however, higher up on no. 12.

No. 13 (Inventory no. ABa 955). Triangular dagger blade with almost straight cutting edges, pronounced midrib and flat butt, slightly sunken in the middle. Two fine rivets (0, 18 cm in D). A burr from the moulding is seen at the top of the blade.
L (along the midrib): 19. 1 cm
Provenance: Melos. Bought by the philologist Mr. Pio in Melos in 1865/66.
Published: (Congres international d'Anthropologie et d'Archeologie prehistorique 1869 (Cph. 1875), 482). Montelius1924, Pl. 7, 4. Dietz 1971, 1 and Fig. 1.
Comments: Renfrew Tp. IVa (Renfrew 1967, 11). Renfrew considers Tp. IVa to be "the principal Aegean form". Nine pieces from Amorgos are catalogued by Renfrew (54-62), furthermore there are parallels from Naxos, Crete and the Mainland, from Zygouries, Lerna and Levkas (Renfrew 1967, 11 (IVa), n. 21). DATING: The Syros/Keros phase in the Cyclades (Renfrew 1972, 517 and 522). The dating is based on daggers from Ormos Apóllonas in Naxos (Papathanasopoulos 1961/62 (1963), Pl. 77-78, gr. 38B) and a piece from Dokathismata gr. 14 in Amorgos (Tsountas 1898, 154, Pl. 12, 8. Bossert 1965, 92f and Abb. 2, 5). Very close parallels from Lebena, Crete Tomb II are dated "not later than EMII") (Alexiou and Warren 2004, 136-37, figs. 36 and 121). Renfrew believes the type to have continued in later times. DISTRIBUTION: Crete and the Cyclades. Renfrew (1967) consider the type to be characteristic even for the Mainland.

No. 14 (Inventory no. 3168/OA VII b 16). Flat, triangular dagger with curved edges and rounded butt with four nail holes on a line along the terminal edge. The two nearest the edge are broken off. An area bordered by a line parallel to the butt towards the blade probably indicates the position of the hilt.
L 20.3 cm
Provenance: Athens. Bought from Heldreich in Athens 1873. Heldreich stated the provenance was Athens.

Published: (Congres international d'Anthropologie et d'Archeologie prehistorique 1869 (Cph. 1875), 482). Worsaae 1879, 346, Fig. 9. Worsaae 1881, 230 and Fig. 9. Montelius 1924. Pl. 7, 9. Dietz 1971, 2 and Fig. 2.
Comments: DATING: A parallel has been found in Prosymna Grave IV (Papadopoulos 1998, 5, no. 2). LHIA (Dietz 1991 passim). DISTRIBUTION: For relations to Italian daggers see Dietz 1971, 5.

No. 15 (Inventory no. 3169/OA VII b 17). Dagger blade with receding cutting edge and flat rhomboid section. "Trapezoid" haft-plate with two rivet-holes at the uppermost part and a rather delicate rivet farther down on the blade. The haft-plate is bent slightly backwards and one edge is damaged. The percentage of tin is rather high (Dietz 1971, 21).
L (middle of the blade): 19.7 cm
Provenance: Athens. Bought from Heldreich 1873, who stated the provenance.
Published: Worsaae 1881, 230, fig. 8. Montelius 1924, Pl. 7,7. Dietz 1971, 2, Fig. 3.
Comments: Renfrew Tp. IVb (Renfrew 1967, 11). DATING: A piece from Lerna (Caskey 1957, Pl. mentions one from the Apeiranthos Museum, Naxos. The type is furthermore known from Crete (The dagger from Athens mentioned by Renfrew 1967, 11, n. 122 is our 3168) and from Albania (Vodhinë, Prendi 2002, Fig 2, 3).

No. 16 (Inventory no. 3150/OA VII b 4). Fragment of a thin, tongue-shaped dagger blade. The upper termination has been cut and the point broken. No midrib marked.
L 13.0 cm. Max. W 3.4 cm
Provenance: Akarnania. Transferred from the "Ethnographical Museum" (The National Museum).
Unpublished.
Comments: A rather similar blade is found in Amorgos (Tsountas 1898, 190, 11 (stray find)) and Syros, Chalandriani, gr. 264 (Tsountas 1898, 103 and 110, Pl. 10, 29). DISTRIBUTION: The Cyclades and the Mainland (?)

No. 17 (Inventory no. 3167/OA. VII b 39) (Fig. 2 Colour photo). Fragmented blade of a dagger. The central part consists of a bronze sheet framed by two parallel double incised lines. The central part is decorated with small hafted gold axes (gold sheet) Four axes are preserved on one side, on the other side traces are preserved of four axes, the gold sheet only preserved in two of them, however.
W (preserved) 3.0 cm. L 19.7 cm. Th. 0.0 cm
Provenance: Thera. Bought from Rhousopoulos in 1873 (R. Christensen 1873 no. 8).
Published: Worsaae 1879, 346 and Pl. 1. Worsaae 1881, 346 and Pl. VIII. Perrot 1886, 347. Perrot et Chipiez 1894, 975 and Fig. 550. Blinkenberg Chr. in Festskrift til H.G. Feilberg 1911, 70. Tsountas-Manatt 1897, 200, 235, Fig. 118. Lamb 1929, 11. Remouchamp 1927, XXXV, note 3. Riis 1957, 27. Vermeule 1964, p. XIIIB. Branigan 1974, 117, note 3. Luce 1969, Pl. 31, p. 91, note 70. GUIDES 1995, 15. Xenaki-Sakellariou and Chatziliou 1989, 28, cat. No. 12, Tf. IX, 1. Laffineur 1974, 11 no. 12. Papadopoulos 1998, 15 (63). Page 1970, 28, Pl. 7a. Dickinson 1977, 83. Higgins 1967, 140.
Comments: DATING: LHI

No. 18 (Inventory no. 3170/OA VII b 37) Narrow, triangular dagger blade with flat, rhomboidal section. Butt damaged, but three closely-located rivet holes placed in a triangle are preserved. No. 18 has a high percentage of tin (Dietz 1971, 21).
L 18. 2 cm
Provenance: Amorgos. Bought from Heldreich in Athens 1873. H. gave Amorgos as the provenance.
Published: Dietz 1971, pp. 5-6 and Fig. 5.
Comments: Considered to be a Syrian dagger (Dietz 1971, 5). DATING: Similar pieces from Crete (Branigan 1968, 60ff). Branigan considered the three-rivet system to derive from Syria and to have inspired Cretan daggers in the transitional period EMIII/MMI. In Syria the type is dated by the "Eneolithic B necropolis" in Byblos to the period after 2250 B.C. (Amiran) corresponding to the end of the EM/EH period in the Aegean (Dietz 1971, 17). A close parallel from Kalymnos, published by Benzi is dated to

EBIII (Benzi 1997, 391, Pl. 4, f. (5937)) DISTRIBUTION: The type – classified as Type VI by Renfrew (1967) – is unusual in the Aegean area. There are two other pieces from the Ashmolean Museum, Oxford with Amorgos as provenance (Renfrew 1967, 11, catalogue nos. 66 and 67, Pls. 7 and 9. See also Sherratt 2000, 83-84 (III.3.13-14), Figs. 42-43 (dating ECII-III transition)). One rather similar piece was found in MH levels in Lerna (Caskey 1957, Pl. 42, c, right). Renfrew refers in general to parallels from Anatolia and Cyprus (Stronach 1957, Tp. 6 and Catling 1964, 60, Fig. 3, 7-11). As for the Palestinian, Cypriot and Syrian parallels, see Dietz 1971, 12-14. Dietz suggested that the types were produced in Byblos or in areas in close contact with Byblos, i.e. Cilicia or Cyprus (Dietz 1971, 6).

No. 19 (Inventory no. 3171/OA VII b 18) Triangular dagger blade with slightly concave cutting edges and rounded midrib. The haft-plate has two rectangular slots in the longitudinal direction of the blade and damaged edges. Butt with a flat, broken off, narrow tang.
L 15,6 cm
Provenance: Athens. Purchased in Athens in 1873 from Heldreich who stated the provenance as Athens.
Published: Worsaae 1879, 346, and Fig. 7. Worsaae 1881, 233 and Fig. 7. Dietz 1971, 5 and Fig. 4. Branigan 1974, 163, Tf. 10, no. 454. Avila 1983, 131, no. 834 ("Lanzenspitze?").
Comments: Renfrew 1967 Type IIa "slotted Daggers/Spearheads without Rat-Tail Tang" (note wrong number in Renfrew 1967, 10, n. 109 (3121 for 3171)). Four pieces in the British Museum and from the Ashmolean, all from Amorgos, are catalogued by Renfrew (nos. 47-50). Also Sherratt 2000, 87-89 (III, 3, 17-18), Figs. 46-47 (dating ECII-III transition)). Others are from Levkas and Troy (Dörpfeld 1927, Pl. 63, 1 and 2. Schmidt 1902, no. 5848). Branigan 1974, Tp. IX. DATING: A piece in a grave from Stavros in Amorgos (Tsountas 1898, Pl. 12, 5) should be dated to Transitional EC/MC or Phylakopi I (iii?) (Dietz 1971, 5). DISTRIBUTION: Renfrew considers the type to be probably of Cycladic origin.

No. 20 (Inventory no. 3191/OA VII b 37). Corroded and fragmentarily preserved triangular dagger blade. The upper termination is partly preserved, the point broken. Four raised, parallel double lines decorate the blade on the sides, two double lines on each side of the slightly raised, oval mid rib and four on the midrib itself.
L 15.6 cm. Max. W 5.1 cm
Provenance: Amorgos. Bought from Rhousopoulos in 1873 (mentioned by R. Christensen).
Published: Worsaae 1879, 343, Fig. 11, 346. Worsaae 1881, 233 and Fig. 10. Branigan 1974 Catalogue no. 195 (7).
Comments: Branigan 1974, 11, "Long Daggers" Tp. X. DATING: The Cretan type is dated to EM/MM.

No. 21 (Inventory no. 3191/OA VIIb 38). Corroded and fragmentarily preserved triangular dagger. The incised upper termination is partly preserved, the point broken. The blade is decorated with raised longitudinal zones with three raised lines in each zone. Slightly raised, oval midrib.
L 14.4 cm. Max. W 3.8 cm
Provenance: Amorgos. Bought from Rhousopoulos 1873 (mentioned by R. Christensen).
Published: Worsaae 1879, 343, Fig. 10, 346. Worsaae 1881, 233 and Fig. 11. Branigan 1974, catalogue no. 195 (7).
Comments: Branigan 1974, 11, "Long Daggers" Tp. X. DATING: The Cretan type is dated to EM/MM.

No. 22 (Inventory no. 3269). Triangular dagger with a semicircular upper termination. Rounded shoulders. The central part of the blade is thickened. Three nails, one in the semicircular tang, two in the shoulders. Well preserved.
L 11.4 cm
Provenance: Arkesine, Amorgos. Found in grave with National Museum, Department of Ancient Cultures of Denmark and the Mediterranean, inventory nos. 3264-3268 (Bossert 1954). Bought in Athens from Palaeologos by Sophus Müller in April-May 1887.
Published: Duemmler 1886, 21, Beilage 1, 7 and Duemmler 1901, 55, Fig. 59. Blinkenberg 1896, 30, Fig. 8. Blinkenberg 1897, 33, Fig. 11. Bossert 1954, 23 ff. Dietz 1971, 17, Fig. 9. Galanakis 2013, Fig. 7, b.

Comments: The unique dagger was found in a cist grave in Arkesine, Western Amorgos. DATING: The context was studied by Eva-Maria Bossert (1954) who suggested a dating contemporary with Phylakopi I.iii/Middle Cycladic (MK) I (2100-1900 BC).

No. 23 (Inventory no. 6884). Dagger with parallel edges. Two nail holes in the upper termination. The upper part broken at the nail holes. Composed of three pieces.
L 23.0 cm
Provenance: Crete (unknown find spot). Gift from the museum in Kandia (Heraklion), 1912.
Unpublished

SPEARHEADS
No. 24 (Inventory no. 1373). Spearhead of bronze. Parts of the slashed socket are missing, however, a small part of the termination is still preserved. The hammered socket has an oval section. The transition between socket and blade is concave. The width of the blade decreases gradually toward the triangular point. The blade with midrib has a rhomboid section. No nail holes.
L 29.1 cm. Max. W at blade 3.1 cm
Provenance: Hypata in Pthiotis. Bought from Heldreich in Athens, May 1880.
Published: Undset 1890, 17, fig. 29.
Comments: Related to Avila, Tp. IV and especially no. 55 from Agh. Ioannis near Knossos (Avila 1983, 26, Tf. 10. This spearhead, however, is longer). DATING: LMIB-II (Agh. Ioannis).

No. 25 (Inventory no. 1642) (See frontpage no. 6). Spearhead of bronze. Part of the slashed socket is missing and no part of the termination remains. The hammered socket has an oval section and a nail hole (D 0.6 cm). Slightly concave, smooth transition to the blade. The blade curves continuously towards the point, the section profiled with flat central part.
L 28. 6 cm
Provenance: Melos. Bought by Sophus Müller in Athens in July 1881.
Unpublished
Comments: Related to Avila Tp. II (Avila 1983, 9-14) but without collar on the socket. DATING: Avila Tp. II belongs mainly to the Shaft Grave Period. The blade on no. 25 resembles Avila no. 17 from "Myrionochorion" with a dating to LHII-IIIA1 (?).

No. 26 (Inventory no. 3173/O.A. VII b 48). Well-preserved spearhead of bronze. Only a small part of the cylindrical, slashed socket is missing. The socket has an outturned collar, decorated with an incised line at the termination. Above this, three incised lines and a fastening hole is placed opposite the slash. The socket continues in the flat blade with an amygdaloid section. The blade is lanceolate and joins the socket at right angles.
L 28.8 cm. Max. W (blade) 2.3 cm
Provenance: Athens. Bought by Sophus Müller in Athens. Fiscal year of 1881-82 (July 1881?).
Unpublished
Comments: Related to Avila 1983, nos. 952-958 (from Olympia and Delphi). DATING: Probably from the Iron Age.

No. 27 (Inventory no. 5602). Bronze spearhead. Repair on the blade and a small part of the edge missing, otherwise completely preserved – but badly corroded. The slashed socket is octagonal with eight facets and two oppositely placed fastening holes, 1,7 cm from the end. The triangular blade is thickened at the centre.
L 35, 2 cm
Provenance: Apollakia, Rhodes. Bought by members of the Lindos campaign in the city of Rhodes in 1903.
Published: LINDOS IV, 1, 77 (fig. 95).

Comments: Höckmann's group F, var. IV (Höckmann 1980, 38, Abb. 7, F 5 from Asklepeion, Kos). The group is characterized by having straight blade edges and an angular transition between blade and socket. The facetted socket is unusual; compare, however, a very similar piece with eight- facetted socket from Eleona, Kos (Morricone 1967, Fig. 62). DATING: LH IIIA2/B. DISTRIBUTION: The group shows an island Aegean distribution with a marked eastern dominance. See also Avila 1983, Tp. IV, Typenreihe C, especially no. 62 (p. 28, Tf. 11) (cit. p. 27ff). Ialysos NT VI (Jacobi 1933, 344f, no 3, Fig. 95 and Ialysos T. 39/4 (Benzi 1992, Tav. 178, d).

No. 28 (Inventory no. 5603). Bronze spearhead. Cut at the lower part of the socket and repaired at the blade and the socket. The socket is almost circular and slashed; evidently the cut runs through the centre of the oppositely placed fastening holes. The lanceolate blade has an amygdaloid section.
L 27. 1 cm
Provenance: Apollakia, Rhodes. Bought by members of the Lindos campaign in the city of Rhodes in 1903.
Published: LINDOS IV, 1, 77 (fig. 96).
Comments: Höckmann's group F, var. IV. DATING: LHIIIA1-LHIIIC. DISTRIBUTION: (see catalogue no. 27) Related specimens from Kos (Morricone 1975, Figs. 63, 65 and 66. Höckmann 1980, F21, F22 and F23). LINDOS IV, 108.

No. 29 (Inventory no. 3191/O.A. VII b 42). Very badly preserved spearhead or lance blade. Broken at the transition between socket and the blade. The socket continues into the blade which was probable rather long and "tongue-shaped". The midrib is pronounced, rhomboid.
L 17.3 cm
Provenance: Thera. Bought from Rhousopoulos in 1873 – who states the provenance Thera. (not mentioned by R. Christensen).
Unpublished
Comments: Probably related to Höckmann 1980, 27 (Var. DI), Abb. 4, D11-13 "…, deren Schneiden… Ganz weich in die Tülle einmunden …". DATING: LHIIA/LMII (Höckmann cit.). The provenance Thera, however, rather indicates a dating not later than LMIA. DISTRIBUTION: Crete and the Peloponnese.

No. 30 (Inventory no. 1643). Spearhead of bronze. Small fragments of the slashed socket are missing but most of the termination is preserved. Slashed, oval socket with two opposed nail holes. Tongue shaped blade with pointed, ovoid section, smooth transition between socket and blade. The socket is longer than the blade.
L15.0 cm
Max. W (socket) 2.1 cm
Provenance: Boiotia. Bought by Sophus Müller in Athens in July 1881.
Unpublished
Comments: Avila 1983, 144, no. 1044, Tf. 51 from Olympia (comp. Weber H. in Kunze E. und Schleif H. OlForsch I, 1944, 150, Tf. 58, c). DATING: LHIII-Early Iron Age.

No. 31 (Inventory no. 3172/O.A. VII b 47) (Fig. frontpage no. 4). Well-preserved spearhead. Small parts of the edges and the point are missing. The socket, with circular section, is cylindrical with a slash, terminating in a band-shaped ring. Two opposed nail holes (d. 0.4 cm) partly cut the ring. The blade is shaped like a bay leaf with a rectangular midrib.
L 22.7 cm. Max. W (blade) 4.0 cm
Provenance: Athens. Bought by Sophus Müller in Athens. Fiscal year of 1881-82 (July 1881?).
Unpublished
Comments: In general, Höckmann 1980, 25f Type D and Avila 1983, 46f, types VII-VIII. For Achaia see Papadopoulos 1979, 164. Papazoglou-Manioudaki 1994a, 182f. DATING: LHIII (LHIIIC in Achaia).

No. 32 (Inventory no. 5669). Spearhead with a lanceolate blade. Part of the socket is missing. The blade has a pronounced square, flat midrib. Two opposed nail holes in the slightly faceted socket.
L 24.8 cm
Provenance: Siana, Rhodes. Bought in Rhodes in 1904 from a dealer who stated that it was found in a Mycenaean grave near Siana in Southern Rhodes (West) together with catalogue numbers 5 and 43.
Published: Sandars 1963, 140, Pl. 27, 55. Dietz and Trolle 1974, 32, Fig. 23. Lambrou-Philipson 1990, Cat. no. 594 and Pl. 81. Avila 1983, 48, no. 104, Tf. 16 (Tp. VII). Höckmann 1980, 31, Abb. 5 (D29).
Comments: "Siana group bronzes" according to Sandars 1963. Höckmann 1980, 31 and 135 (Variant III). DATING: LHIIIB-C (according to Sandars 1963). Also Klauss (Antheia) (Papadopoulos and Kontorli-Papadopoulos 1984, 221-224 with a suggested dating in LHIIIC). DISTRIBUTION: Peloponnese and the Eastern Aegean (Höckmann cit.).

No. 33 (Inventory no. 1374). Spearhead of bronze. Parts of the blade and shaft are missing. The circular socket continues on the blade in the form of a sharp central ridge. The blade is pointed oval.
L 13.8 cm
Provenance: Kythera. Bought from Heldreich, Athens May 1880.
Unpublished

No. 34 (Inventory no. 1375 (a)). Spearhead of bronze. Slightly damaged oval socket with two nail holes. Clearly visible line where the hammered sheet joins the socket. The long oval blade is flat in the central axis.
L 13.9 cm
Provenance: Crete. Bought from Heldreich in Athens May 1880
Unpublished
Comments: Compare Höckmann 1980, 25 and 134, Abb. 4 (D10) (Malthi). DATING: MHIII/MMIII. DISTRIBUTION: Crete and the Peloponnese (Höckmann cit.)

No. 35 (Inventory no. 1375 (b)). Spearhead (or arrowhead!) of bronze. The conical socket, with two nail holes, was produced by hammering the metal sheet. The pointed oval blade has a central flat part in the central axes.
L 10.5 cm
Provenance: Crete
Published: Undset 1890, 17, Fig. 30.
Comments: Compare Höckmann 1980, Abb. 3 (C13) (Knossos). DATING: SMII. DISTRIBUTION: Crete and the Peloponnese (Höckmann cit.).

KNIVES
No. 36 (Inventory no. 12413). Bronze knife with one cutting edge. Only a few fragments are missing. Straight transition to the handle zone (L 6, 4 cm) with three nail holes. The thick back of the blade curves slightly.
L 28.0 cm
Provenance: Apsaktiras, Rhodes ("grave 1").
Published: LINDOS IV, 1, 58 (Fig. 62) (no. 11).
Comments: Sandars Type1b.Ialysos NT 59 (Maiuri 1926, 149, Fig. 147 and Benzi 1992, 177, 360, Tav. 179, i). Sandars Type 1 knives are most recently discussed by Alram-Stern and Deger-Jalkotzy 2006, 105f. DATING: LHIIIA-B (Lindos IV, 105). Alram-Stern (cit.) indicates a dating from the Shaft Grave Period to "IIIC Früh-Entwickelt" for the Type 1 in general. DISTRIBUTION: European connections are discussed by Harding 1975, 197 and Benzi cit. Alram-Stern includes Cyprus and Southern Italy in the distribution pattern of Type 1.

No. 37 (Inventory no. 12414). Bronze knife with one cutting edge. Part of the edge and the point missing. The flat handle zone (4.7 cm in length), with a convex termination, is clearly indicated and fragments of the originally organic cover are still preserved. Two nails are still in situ. The curving blade has a thick back and evidently the point turned upwards.

L 22.5 cm

Provenance: Apsaktiras, Rhodes. Gift from the Carlsberg Foundation.

Published: LINDOS IV, 1 58 (no. 9), Fig. 62.

Comments: The knife should in general be included in Sandars Type 1a (see also comments to catalogue nos. 40-41). The short handle zone (proportion between handle zone and blade 1:3) must indicate that the piece was not used as an ordinary knife. The s-curved outline is found on a (Sandars Type 1b) knife from the Dictaean Cave (Boardman 1961, 20, Fig. 4, 70) and from Kos (Morricone 1975, 278 (no. 3), fig. 239 (Sandars Type. 1b)). Milojcic considered the curving blade to show Central European affinities (Milojcic 1955, 156). DATING: See in general nos. 36 and 40.

No. 38 (Inventory no. 7700). Bronze knife with evenly-curved, thickened back and curved edge. The handle zone, which has three nail-holes (only two nails are preserved), has very low flanges. The blade has evidently been sharpened.

L 18.3 cm

Provenance: Ta Tzingani, Rhodes. Excavated by K.F. Kinch August 1, 1908.

Published: LINDOS IV, 1, 85 (Fig. 108).

Comments: Sandars Type 1b. DATING: LHIIIA (from the grave).

No. 39 (Inventory no. 12416). Bronze knife with one cutting edge. The top of the handle is broken. The handle zone (L 4.0 cm) is clearly marked, flat with sporadically slightly raised edges. Three nails of which two are preserved. The slightly thick back of the blade curves somewhat – the edge has evidently been sharpened.

L 15.1 cm

Provenance: Apsaktiras, Rhodes.

Published: LINDOS IV, 1, 58 (Fig. 62) (no. 10).

Comments: Sandars Type 1a. Compare a knife from Crete (Milojcic 1955, 155, Abb. 1, 2) dated by Milojcic to the period between 1250 and 950 BC. Tinos, Agh. Theklas (Despini 1979 (1981), 232-235, Pl 143). DATING: The type probably dates LH IIIA2 to IIIC.

No. 40 (Inventory no. 12415). One-edged bronze knife. The termination of the short, flanged grip is slightly convex. One rivet hole and two rivets in the flange. Traces of a pale yellow organic covering, probably ivory, are preserved on both sides of the flange. The blade is rather flat and slightly curved. The back is thickened.

L 13.8 cm. W 1.3 cm

Provenance: Passia Grave 2, Rhodes. Gift from the Carlsberg Foundation.

Published: LINDOS IV, 1, 35 (2, 8), Fig. 28.

Comments: Sandars Type 1a (Sandars 1955, 175 ff, Catling 1968, 107 and LINDOS IV, 1, 100). DATING: LHIIIB/C (see also catalogue nos. 36 and 37).

No. 41 (Inventory no. 3152/O.A. VII b 6). One-edged knife, straight back, curving at the point. Except for a break in the handle zone right through a nail hole, completely preserved.

L 11.5 cm

Provenance: "Thebe" (Thebes). Purchased in 1873 from Rhousopoulos in Athens. Mentioned by R. Christensen in Febr. 1873 (provenance said to be Thebe).

Unpublished

Comments: Sandars Type.1a (Sandars 1955, 175). See also Alram-Stern 2006, 105-106. DATING: LH (I-IIIC) (Alram-Stern cit.). DISTRIBUTION: (Sandars Tp. 1a): The Aegean, the Dodecanese, Cyprus, Anatolia and the Levant (Sandars 1955, 177) and Southern Italy (Alram-Stern 2006 cit.).

No. 42 (Inventory no. 3151/O.A. VII b 5). One-edged knife. Straight back. Two out of three bronze nails are still preserved in the handle zone. Slightly damaged at the point.
L 12.8 cm
Provenance: Thebe. Purchased in 1873 from Rhousopoulos in Athens. Mentioned by R. Christensen, February, 1873 (from Thebe).
Published: Worsaae 1879, 346, 343 and Fig. 6. Worsaae 1881, 233, 230 and Fig. 6.
Comments: Ref. catalogue no. 41.

No. 43 (Inventory no. 5670). One-edged bronze knife with missing point and some damage at the edge – otherwise preserved. The handle zone with high flanges and partly-preserved bone inlay terminates in a square tang (for a pommel?). The thickened back of the blade is slightly curved.
L 30.5 cm
Provenance: Siana, Rhodes. Bought in Rhodes in 1904 from a dealer who stated it had been found in a Mycenaean grave near Siana in Southern Rhodes (West) together with catalogue numbers 5 and 22.
Published: Sandars 1963, 140 ff ("Siana group bronzes"), Pl. 27, no. 54. Dietz and Trolle 1974, 32, Fig. 23, th.
Comments: See below catalogue no. 44.

No. 44 (Inventory no. 12417). Bronze knife with one cutting edge. Fragments missing from the blade and the haft. The handle zone (L 10, 0 cm (point included)) framed by raised edges, terminates in a long square point. Fragments of an organic inlay can be seen, no nail holes visible. The curving blade has a thick back and the edge has probably been sharpened.
L (preserved) 26.4 cm
Provenance: Apsaktiras, Rhodes. Gift from the Carlsberg Foundation.
Published: LINDOS IV, 1, 58 (fig. 62) (no. 12).
Comments: The knife belongs to Sandars "Siana group" and is especially close to the knife from Siana itself (See catalogue no. 43. Sandars 1963, 140 ff. and Sandars 1978, 158, Figs. 106-110). DATING: Considered by Sandars to be inspired by Levantine prototypes and to be dated in the 12th century B.C. A dating in LHIIIA/B, however, seems more likely (LINDOS IV, 1, 105). Also Mee 1982, 60. DISTRIBUTION: Restricted to the Eastern Aegean: Ialysos, Colophon, Fraktin, Troy and Armenochori in Astypalia (Mee 1982, 60. LINDOS IV, 1, 105). A dagger from Igdebaglari hoard in the Marmaris has the same handle zone with high flanges and terminates in a square tang (Buchholz 1999, 90, Fig. 25c (with reference to Harmankaya N.S. in Reading in Prehistory, Studies presented to Halet Cambel, 1995, 232, Abb. 17).

No. 45 (Inventory no. 4673) (see front page no.1). One-edged knife. The blade is flat, slightly thicker at the haft. Out of the three nail-holes, one still retains its nail.
L 17.2 cm
Provenance: Amorgos. Bought by Chr. Blinkenberg on a journey to Italy and Greece during the spring of 1896 from Palaeologos in Athens. Provenance stated, with safety, to be from Amorgos (Ref. Introduction). Compare also catalogue no. 68. Others were found in 1896 (probably from Tsountas' excavations).
Published: K. Branigan 1974, 167, no. 656 (13).
Comments: Sandars Type. 6b (Sandars 1955, 183). Branigan 1974, 167, no. 656 (13), "Knives" Tp. V. The various types of this knife are, most recently, treated in Kilian-Dirlmeier 1997, 50-53. DATING: Knives with straight back are dated MHII-MHIII. At the transition to Mycenaean the back becomes curved as no. 45 (Kilian-Dirlmeier 1997, 52). Our knife is included in Kilian-Dirlmeier Variante 1 with DISTRIBUTION: Chora (Kephalovryson, Messenia), Lerna, Asine, Theben, Sesklo, Dodona, Amorgos, Mykene (Shaftgrave A, VI), Prosymna, Iglarevo (Kosovo) and Aigina. See also Dietz 1980, 85-86.

DOUBLE-AXES
No. 46 (Inventory no. 3158/O.A. VII b 45). Almost symmetrical axe of bronze with circular shaft hole. Entirely preserved except for the edges which are slightly damaged.
L 19.8 cm. D of shaft hole: 2.3 cm
Provenance: Akarnania. Bought in Athens 1880. Fiscal year 1880-81.

Published: Worsaae 1879, 342, 343 and Fig. 1. Worsaae 1881, 233, 230 and Fig. 1. Montelius 1924, Pl. 5, 8. Buchholz 1959, 46 (II,2c) Typ II, Tf. IXa. Mentioned in Buchholz 1983, 72.
Comments: See Buchholz 1959. DATING: LM III.

No. 47 (Inventory no. 3156/O.A. VI b 30). Almost symmetrical double-axe with circular shaft hole.
L 22.8 cm. D of shaft hole: 3.5 cm
Provenance: Naxos. Bought from Rhousopoulos in Athens in 1873.
Published: Worsaae 1879, 346, 343 and fig. 2. Worsaae 1881, 233, 230 and Fig. 2. Montelius 1924, Pl. 5,10. Buchholz 1959, 49 (II,14d) Typ II, Tf. X, e.
Comments: Comstock and Vermeule1971, p. 392, no. 538. DATING: LM III.

No. 48 (Inventory no. 1323). Asymmetrical double-axe of bronze with curved upper and lower sides. Circular shaft-hole placed approximately 1/3 from one end. Entirely preserved.
L 17.2 cm. D of shaft hole: 3.5 cm.
Provenance: Akarnania. Bought in Athens from Heldreich in November 1879. Stated to be from Akarnania.
Unpublished
Comments: "SE Europe"?

No. 49 (Inventory no. 3157/O.A. VII b 3). Almost symmetrical double-axe of bronze with circular shaft hole. Entirely preserved.
L 21.0 cm. D of shaft hole: 3.8 cm.
Provenance: Naxos. Bought in the fiscal year of 1871-1872. Bought from Rhousopoulos 1873 in Athens.
Published: Buchholz 1959, 49 (II,14e) Type II (not depicted).
Comments: DATING: LMIII (Buchholz cit.).

No. 50 (Inventory no. 3160/O.A. VII b 26). Almost symmetrical double axe of bronze incurved at the shaft hole. Oval shaft hole with incurved sides and grooves along the blade. The axe is entirely preserved except for the one edge which is damaged.
L 14.5 cm. Max. Th 2.2 cm
Provenance: Peloponnese. Bought from Rhousopoulos in 1873 (not mentioned by R. Christensen).
Published: Branigan 1974, 165, cat. No. 538 (12) (double axes tp. IIa).
Comments: Ref. "Tsountas' hoard", Mycenae (Spyropoulos 1972, Figs. 1-9). Ialysos NT 70 (Benzi 1992, 377, 16. Tav. 180i). DATING: LHIIIB/C. DISTRIBUTION: See Benzi 1992, 180.

No. 51 (Inventory no. 1325). Almost symmetrical shaft-hole axe with circular shaft hole. Entirely preserved.
L 12.2 cm. D of shaft-hole: 3.5 cm
Provenance: Akarnania. Bought from Heldreich in November 1879.
Published: Buchholz 1959, 46 (II, 2b). Typ II (not depicted) and Buchholz 1983, 72.
Comments: See Buchholz 1959. DATING: LM III.

No. 52 (Inventory no. 1324). Symmetrical double-axe of bronze with almost parallel upper and lower sides. Circular shaft hole with grooves in the longitudinal axes of the axe. Entirely preserved except for a part of the one edge missing.
L 14.5 cm. D of shaft hole: 2.8 cm
Provenance: Akarnania. Bought in Athens from Heldreich in November 1879.
Unpublished: Mentioned in Buchholz 1959, 46 (II,2a) Typ I/II (not depicted) and Buchholz 1983, 72.
Comments: See Buchholz 1959. DATING: LM III.

No. 53 (3169/O.A. VII b 51) (see front page no.15). Symmetrical double axe of bronze with oval shaft hole and collar on the lower (or upper?) side. The surface in its original colour without patina. Slightly damaged at the edges.

L 18.1 cm. Max. D of shaft hole: 2.6 cm.

Provenance: Naxos. Bought by Sophus Müller in Greece in the fiscal year 1881-1882 (July 1881).

Published: Branigan 1974, 165, cat. No. 547 (12) ("Double-Axes" Tp. IV). Buchholz 1960, p. 51, fig. 6a. Buchholz 1983, 89 (no. 14), Fig. 23, c.

Comments: "North Greek-Southern Albanian double-axe variant Type "Kierion"" (Kilian 1976, 121, Abb. 7 and Kilian 1986, 287, Fig. 11). Extensive catalogue in Buchholz 1983, 83-90: "Doppeltäxte mit Tüllenwulst an der Oberseite" ("Hermonetyp" und Varianten") and Figs. 23-24. DATING: An unpublished very close parallel from Aghias Mammas, level 7 in Macedonia is dated to LHI-LHIIA (Bernhard Hänsel personal information). DISTRIBUTION: Distribution map in Buchholz 1983, Fig. 22 and 26 ("dalmatinisch-epeirotischer Types …". To this should be added the double axe from Aghias Mamas in Macedonia mentioned above. Also Buchholz 1999, 92 and Fig. 27, a and Albania, (Prendi 2002, Fig. 4, 11. Nepravishtë).

No. 54 (Inventory no. 6883). Symmetrical double axe in bronze with circular shaft hole. Entirely preserved.

L 16.6 cm

D of shaft hole: 2.5 cm

Provenance: Selakano, Crete. Gift from the Museum in Heraklion 1912.

Unpublished

Comments: Minoan type related to Buchholz 1959, 39, Tf. V, b-d, same in Buchholz 1983, Abb. 8b. Also Buchholz 1959, 40, Tf. VI, c (Palaikastro). DATING: LMII.

SOCKETED AXES

No. 55 (Inventory no. 3153/O.A. VII b 31). One-edged hammer-axe in bronze. The button butt consists of an almost circular knob. Broad curved edge. The broad sides are facetted and the narrow sides are angular around the circular shaft hole. Entirely preserved.

L 17.2 cm. H at shaft hole: 2.3 cm. H of edge: 7.9 cm

Provenance: Naxos. Bought from Rhousopoulos in 1873.

Published: Montelius 1924, Pl. 4, 8. Branigan 1974, 166, no. 585 (13) ("Single-axes" Type II). Lesley Fitton 1989, 36, Fig. 2. Chantre 1874, 7f, fig. 2-3.

Comments: Renfrew 1967, 8 f. compared the axe to one in the British Museum from the so-called "Kythnos hoard" (Renfrew 1967, Cat. no. 11, DM 66, 2-7, 8). In 1989 Lesley Fitton convincingly argued that the hoard, of which 8 pieces are in the British Museum and four in Copenhagen (See also Catalogue nos. 63, 64 and 67), was found in Naxos (Now called "the new Naxos hoard"). Both groups were bought from Rhousopoulos (Lesley Fitton 1989, passim). DATING: Dated by Renfrew to EB2. See however Lesley Fitton 1989, 35-36. A dating in the Early Bronze Age is still the more likely. DISTRIBUTION: Renfrew considers the type to be unusual ("So far the form is uniquely Cycladic", Renfrew 1967, 9). Sinclair Hood, visiting the museum in Copenhagen in March 1958 considers the piece to be Middle European. Middle European parallels in comp. Coll. National Museum – in stone (battle axes?).

No. 56 (Inventory no. 3155/O.A. VII.b.50). One-edged axe with pointed back and large, asymmetrical, "bearded", curved edge. Circular shaft hole.

L 8.1 cm. Max. Th: 2.7 cm

Provenance: Not stated. Bought by Sophus Müller in Greece in July 1881.

Published: Branigan 1974, 165, no. 562 (12). "Picks" Type I.

Comments: "Professor Gordon Childe visiting the museum in 1938 considered the piece to be South Russian".

No. 57 (Inventory no. 1646). Bronze axe with circular shaft hole placed towards the termination with short, narrow, rather straight butt. The cutting edge is curved. Grooves are seen on the upper side of the blade on each side of the slightly oval shaft hole.

L 17.4 cm. Th at shaft hole: 4.2 cm

Provenance: Ikaría. Bought by Sophus Müller in Athens in July 1881.

Published: Branigan 1974, 165, cat. No. 549 (12) ("Double-axes" Type V).

Comments: DATING: From the Urnfield period to Hallstatt Zeit (Žeravica 1993, 44 f, Tf. 12). DISTRI-BUTION: "Mitteldalmatien" (Žeravica 1993, nos. 111-123). Mainly Italy but also former Yoguslavia ("Mitteldalmatien"), Steirmark and other parts of Austria.

No. 58 (Inventory no. 3154/VII b 49). One-edged hammer-axe in bronze. Narrow, flat hammer at back, curved, broad edge in front. The axe in square around the circular shaft hole. Curving in the longitudinal axes. Completely preserved.

L 14.0 cm

The back (hammer) measures: 3.9x2.4 cm. The curved edge: 5.2 cm

Provenance: Lebadea. Bought by Sophus Müller in Greece in July 1881 (fiscal year 1881-82).

Published: Branigan 1974, 165, no. 559 (12) ("Axe-Hammers" Type I).

Comments: DATING: Final Neolithic/Chalcolithic. Žeravica 1993, 5-6, nos.2-4, Tf. 1: 2-4. "Hammeräxte von Typ. Pločnik". Chalcolithic/Final Neolithic (Zachos 2010 cit.)/Cucuteni (A3), Tiszapolgar (Vulpe 1975, 20-21) or typ Vidra (Vulpe 1975, Tf. 2, 24) – same dating. DISTRIBUTION: For a similar axe from Mesolonghi see Zachos 2010, 86, Fig. 6-6, γ (BSA collection, Athens) (Chalcolithic/Final Neolithic). Middle-North Serbia et al. (Žeravica 1993, 6) Rumania (Vulpe 1975, 21), Bulgaria (Karanova VI/Varna) (Todorova 1981, 31 ff, Tf. 6).

No. 59 (Inventory no. 1645) (see front page no. 13). Bronze axe with facetted body and circular shaft hole near the rounded termination. Curved edge. Well preserved.

L 13.1 cm. D of shaft hole: 5.1 cm.

Provenance: Spata, Attica. Bought by Sophus Müller in Athens in July 1881.

Published: Branigan 1974, 166 no. 577 (12) ("Single-axes" Type I).

Comments: DATING: "… Die Ansatz in die Zeit der Vucedoler Kultur". Related to Žeravica 1993, 21, Tf. 5: 45 ("Tp. Corbasca" (Montenegro)) (3rd Millenium BC).

AXE/ADZE

No. 60 (Inventory no. 1326) (see front page no.11). Axe-adze of bronze with vertical edge and horizontal edge on back. Circular shaft hole with pointed collar on the lower side.

L 14.8 cm. D of shaft hole: 3.4 cm

Provenance: Akarnania. Bought from Heldreich in Athens in November 1879.

Unpublished.

Comments: Renfrew 1967 considered a similar piece in the British Museum to be from the "Kythnos hoard" (Renfrew 1967, 8) while Lesley Fitton (1989, 35) excluded it from the context. A convincing parallel was found in an EHII hoard in Eutresis (Goldman 1931, Fig. 287, 2). DATING: EHII.

FLAT AXES/CHISELS

No. 61 (Inventory no. 1644). Flat axe with narrow back widening towards the edge.

L 20.5 cm. Th 0.7 cm

Provenance: Leucas. Bought in Athens 1881.

Published: Branigan 1974, 169, no.781 (15), chisels Type III.

Comments: DATING: The axe is related to the flat axes from the Petralona hoard in Chalkidiki dated to the early half of the 3rd mill. BC (EH II). Grammenou and Tzaxili 1994, 78-81. Figs. 1-4 and Maran 2001, passim (Late EHI/early EHII). DISTRIBUTION: See Grammenou and Tzaxili 1994.

No. 62 (Inventory no. 1359). Chisel of bronze. Well preserved.

L 15.2 cm. Th: 1.1 cm

Provenance: Akarnania. Bought from Heldreich, Athens in April 1880.

Unpublished

Comments: Ref. Spyropoulos 1972, 69 (α-δ). figs. 128-131 and Tf. 20-21 (From the Acropolis hoard, Athens). idem. p. 22 and Figs. 21-30, Pl. 9-10 (From Tsountas' hoard from Mycenae). DATING: LHIIIB/C.

No. 63 (Inventory no. 3145/O.A. VII b 33). Flat chisel. Battered back.
L (preserved) 18.0 cm. Weight: 220 gr. (Lesley Fitton 1989, 36)
Provenance: Naxos. Bought from Rhousopoulos in 1873.
Published: Worsaae 1879, 346, 343 and Fig. 3. Branigan 1974, 169, no. 790 (15) ("Chisels Type III"). Lesley Fitton 1989, 36, Fig. 2.
Comments: See Catalogue no. 55. A piece from the Ashmolean see Sherratt 2000, 72 (III, 3, 1), Fig. 30, said to be from Amorgos (dating ECII?). DATING: EB.

No. 64 (Inventory no. 3144/O.A. VII b 32) (see front page no. 8). "Flat axe with square perforation. Battered cutting edge, hammered equally on both faces" (cit. Lesley Fitton 1989, 36).
L 17.3 cm. Max. Th 1.0 cm. Weight. 600 gr. (Lesley Fitton 1989, 36)
Provenance: Naxos. Bought from Rousopoulos in 1873.
Published: Branigan 1969, 6 and note 30. Branigan 1974, 166, no. 615 (13) ("Flat-axes" Type III). Lesley Fitton 1989, 36, Fig. 2.
Comments: See Catalogue no. 67. DATING: EB.

No. 65 (Inventory no. 3146/O.A. VII.b.46?). Chisel of bronze. Battered back. Damaged.
L 17.6. Th 0.7 cm
Provenance: Leukas. Bought by Sophus Müller in 1881 (fiscal year 1881-82).
Published: Branigan 1974, 169. No. 782 (14) ("Chisels Type III").

No. 66 (Inventory no. 3147). Flat chisel of bronze. Broken at both ends.
L (preserved) 18.5 cm. Th 0.6 cm. Max. W 2.7 cm
Provenance: Thera. Probably from Rhousopoulos 1873.
Published: Branigan 1974, 169, no. 752 (14) ("Chisels type II").
Comments: DATING: MH/LHI.

No. 67 (Inventory no. 3143/O.A. VII b 32). "Flat axe with square perforation. Cutting edge in good condition, hammered equally on both faces" (cit. Lesley Fitton 1989, 36).
L 19.7 cm. Th 0.9 cm. Weight 720 gr. (Lesley Fitton 1989, 36)
Provenance: Naxos. Bought from Rousopoulos 1873. R. stated the provenance.
Published: Lesley Fitton 1989, 36 and fig. 2. Branigan 1969, 6, note 30. Branigan 1974, no. 616 (13).
Comments: See also comments to Catalogue no. 55. Probably from "the new Naxos hoard" (Lesley-Fitton 1989 passim). DATING: EB.

CHISELS
No. 68 (Inventory no. 4674) (see fron page no. 10). Flat chisel of bronze. The curved, "bearded" edge is placed asymmetrically (closer to the underside). The back is broader than the blade. Well preserved.
L 16.3 cm
Provenance: Amorgos. Bought by Blinkenberg on a journey during the spring of 1896 from Palaeologos. (ref. introduction).
Published: Branigan 1974, 170, no. 793 (14) ("Chisels Type III").
Comments: Compare Renfrew 1967, 8, no. 37. DATING: EC.

No. 69 (Inventory no. 3191/O.A. VII.b.34). Flat chisel. Damaged.
L (preserved) 7.2 cm. Max. W 3 cm
Provenance: Naxos. Bought from Rhousopoulos in 1873 (not mentioned by R. Christensen). Labelled: "Naxou".

Comments: The following numbers are included in Inventory no. 3191: O.A. VII.b.21, 34, 37, 38, 41, 42 and a fragmentarily preserved bronze dagger. Dating:?

No. 70 (Inventory no. 3148/O.A. VII b 15). Flat chisel of bronze. The one end is triangular, pointed, the other end shows a curving, horizontal edge. Well preserved.
L. 13.7 cm
Provenance: Attika. Bought from Rhousopoulos in 1873.
Published: Worsaae 1879, 346, 343 and Fig. 4. Worsaae 1881, 233, 230 and Fig. 4. Branigan 1974, 170, no. 916 (15) ("Chisels Type V").

VARIOUS
No. 71 (Inventory no. 1444). Double hammer of bronze. Square shaft hole. The flat surfaces are slightly concave, probably caused by blows. Well preserved.
L 6.2 cm. The ends measure: 2,7x3,0 cm
Provenance: Near Athens. Bought from Heldreich in Athens in October 1880.
Unpublished
Comments: DATING: LH ("Bronze Récent") (Deshayes 1960, 296 f., n.7, no. 2310, Tp. A1a. From Mycenae and Enkomi).

No. 72 (Inventory no. 5601). Bronze razor having a simple square handle with three nail holes – two nails preserved (however all three nails were extant earlier). Part of the blade missing and the handle repaired.
L 18.5 cm
Provenance: Apollakia, Rhodes. Purchased by members of the Lindos excavations team in the city of Rhodes in 1903.
Published: LINDOS IV, 1, 77 (fig. 94)
Comments: Common Aegean triangular type of razor with curved edge (Sandars 1958-59, 235). Closest parallels from Ialysos are from graves 48/14 and 59/D (Benzi 1992, 333-334 and 360, Tav. 121. In general pp. 178-179). Also from Langada, Kos, tomb 25 (Morricone 1967, 150). DATING: LH IIIA2.

No. 73 (Inventory no. 3149/O.A. VII b 24). Sickle of bronze. The rectangular haft has a circular hole toward the end. The blade has a triangular section, somewhat battered toward the point.
L 25.7 cm
Provenance: Corinth. Bought from Rhousopoulos in 1873.
Published: Worsaae 1879, 346, 344 and Fig.5. Worsaae 1881, 233, 231 and Fig. 5.
Comments: Ref. Spyropoulos 1972, 25ff., Figs. 35-53 and Pls. 10-11 (From Tsountas' hoard in Mycenae). The sickle belongs to Catling tp. Ea and Deshayes tp. D2b with a long blade. See most recently Alram-Stern in Alram-Stern und Deger-Jalkotzy 2006, 106-108. DATING: "LHIIIB Ende to LHIIIC Fortgeschritten" (Alram-Stern cit.). DISTRIBUTION: The Greek Mainland.

No. 74 (Inventory no. 3189/O.A. VII b 14). Bronze fish hook. The hook, without barb, is pointed, the tang is flat. Blows from a hammer where the hook is turned. Well preserved.
L 6.0 cm
Provenance: Athens. Bought from Rhousopoulos in 1873 (no provenance stated in the Ethnographical Museum records).
Unpublished
Comments: DATING: Bronze Age.

No. 75 (Inventory no. 12381). Bronze arrowhead. The blade is asymmetrical, one side is straight, the other convex. The straight one is broken at the bottom. The convex side terminates at the foot in a slight hook. The mid part of the blade is thickened, this thickening continuing in the upper part of the point which, at the bottom, tends to be slimmer with a pointed oval section.
L 5.1 cm

Provenance: Passia Grave 2, Rhodes. Gift from the Carlsberg Foundation to the National Museum.
Published: LINDOS IV, 1, 35 (2, 9), Fig. 29.
Comments: DATING: LHIIIB/C by context (LINDOS IV, 100).

No. 76 (Inventory no. 12394). Copper or bronze (not gold) foil with rosette pattern. Eight petals round a circular centre in relief. Tracing of casting at the centre of the reverse.
D 1.5 cm
Provenance: Apsaktiras, Rhodes. Gift from the Carlsberg Foundation.
Published: LINDOS IV, 1, 59 (no. 2) Fig. 63.
Comments: DATING: Bronze Age.

No. 77 (Inventory no. 7701). Fish hook of bronze with barb. The tang is flat (hammered?) while the wire for the hook has a circular section.
L 4.5 cm
Provenance: Kattavia. Rhodes.
Published: LINDOS IV, 1, 85 and Fig. 109.
Comments: Iakovidis tp. 2 (Perati II, 354, Fig. 156, M 73). Buchholz, Jöhrens, Maull 1973, 171, Fig. 55, f and g. Two pieces from Ialysos (T15/28A and B. Benzi 1992, 254, Tav. 181, l, m). DATING: IIIA2-IIIC (Benzi 1992, 179 ff.).

No. 78 (Inventory no. 12380). Ribbon-shaped finger ring in bronze.
D (inner) 1.6 cm
Provenance: Passia Grave 2, 7 Rhodes. Gift from the Carlsberg Foundation.
Published: LINDOS IV, 1, 35, Fig. 27.
Comments: Finger rings are unusual in Mycenaean graves from the Dodecanese. DATING: LHIIC (early) (LINDOS IV, 1, 100).

No. 79 (Inventory no. 3191) Flat object of bronze with raised rim.
L 6.0 cm. W 1.2 cm. H 0.9 cm
Provenance: Athens. Bought from Rhousopoulos in 1873 (with a label giving provenance as. Athens). Transferred from the Ethnographical Museum 1886 (Old no. 21).
Unpublished
Comments: Unfinished small spearhead??

BRACELETS
No. 80 (Inventory no. ABa 319). Bracelet in bronze with circular section. The ends terminate in globular knobs. Decoration inside the knobs with 2 by 4 incised, parallel lines. Well preserved.
D 9.2 cm
Provenance: Unknown. Bought by C.T. Falbe in Greece ("brought from Athens"). The inventory no. derives from the Royal Collection (?) 1844/45.
Published: Breitenstein 1951, 108.
Comments: DATING: "Pre-Mycenaean" according to Breitenstein.

No. 81 (Inventory no. 285). Bracelet in bronze in the shape of a spiral. The inside is flat, the outside curved. Well preserved.
"cross-section": 0.5 cm
Provenance: Unknown. Bought in Athens from Professor Heldreich in March 1870.
Unpublished
Comments: DATING: LHIIIC (Perati. Iakovidis 1969/70).

No. 82 (Inventory no. 1442). Bracelet in bronze. The spiral is made of a thick bronze band with midrib on both in–and outside (most pronounced on the outside). Well preserved.
D 9.0 cm
Provenance: Thessaloniki. Bought from Heldreich in Athens in October 1880 (stated to have been found near Thessaloniki).
Unpublished
Comments: DATING: LH (Catling 1964, 232, no. 6 (Nicosia-Lapithos (LCII)).

No. 83 (Inventory no. 7754). Bracelet in bronze in the shape of a spiral formed by a 1.0 to 1.3 cm broad thin band with a faint midrib on the outside. One end is broken; the other end is thickened (3 cm).
D 6.0 to 7.5 cm
Provenance: Macedonia. From Kinch's collection in 1921 "Objects from Macedonia".
Unpublished
Comments: DATING: Iron Age, 9th century BC. (Andronikos 1969). DISTRIBUTION: Central European origin (Andronikos 1969, 241, 243, Figs. 83, 86γ, 88α, 91v, 94i, 99θ et. al.).

VARIOUS OBJECTS IN GOLD AND SILVER
No. 84 (Inventory no. 4675). Bracelet of silver consisting of a 1.2-1.8 cm hammered broad band. The band has a concavity on the inner side while the outside curves outwards. At the slightly narrowing ends there is a zone with a cross-hatch decoration. Entirely preserved.
D 6.9 cm (max.)
Provenance: Amorgos. Bought in 1896 in Athens.
Published: Renfrew 1967, Pl. 1, 8 (?)
Comments: The piece is mentioned by Renfrew 1967, 6. Another one is kept in the Ashmolean (Renfrew 1967, 18, cat. No. 8 (AE253). Sherratt 2000, 96 (III,4,1) (with dating "probably ECII)). Branigan 1974, 187, no. 2545 (21) ("Bangles" Type III). Also Barber 1987, 105, Fig. 79 from the Dokathismata cemetery, Amorgos (Tsountas 1898, 155, Pl. 8, 2). DATING: ECII.

No. 85 (Inventory no. 3263). Awl in bronze with square section and handle in green anhydrite or calcite.
L 14.1 cm (shaft included)
Provenance: Amorgos. Bought by Sophus Müller from Palaeologos in April/May 1887.
Published: Duemmler 1886, 20, Beilage 1 (D2). Blinkenberg 1896, 43f, Fig. 10. Blinkenberg 1897, 48f, Fig. 14. Branigan 1974, 199, no. 3354. Galanakis 2013, Fig. 10, b.
Comments: Catalogue no. 85 is mentioned in Renfrew 1967, 67 (note 65). Similar piece from Kapros in Amorgos, Renfrew 1967, 6 Pl. 4, 20. (Catalogue no. 20 from the Ashmolean Museum, Oxford). DATING: EC2 (Duemmler's Kapros group. Renfrew 1967, 6 and Renfrew 1972, 522 f. (Keros-Syros phase)). Sherratt 2000, 42 (1.a.7) and Fig. 2 (ECI-II transition (Kampos grp.)).

No. 86 (Inventory no. 12394). Piece of thin gold foil, fragmentarily preserved. Pattern of eight grooved lines radiating from a circular grooved centre. Two perforations for fixing at the edge of the central groove.
D 2.5 cm
Provenance: Apsaktiras, Rhodes. Gift from the Carlsberg Foundation.
Published: LINDOS IV, 1, 60 (no. 3), Fig. 63.
Comments: DATING: LHIIIA2-C.

No. 87 (Inventory no. 12396) (not depicted). Small, cylindrical, granulated (?) gold bead with thread hole.
H 0,3 cm
Provenance: Apsaktiras, Rhodes. Gift from the Carlsberg Foundation.
Published: LINDOS IV, 1, 59, Fig. 63 (no. 1)
Comments: Simple variant of usual type. See for instance from the Tiryns hoard (Spyropoulos 1972, Pl. 27). See also LINDOS IV, 1, 105. DATING: LHIIIA2-C.

No. 88 (Inventory no. 12408). Silver finger-ring with an oval bezel terminating centrally in a point.
Ribbon shaped ring
Oval sheet 2.2x1.6 cm
Provenance: Passia Grave 2, Rhodes. Gift from the Carlsberg Foundation.
Published: LINDOS IV, 1, 35 (2, 6), Fig. 26.
Comments: DATING: LHIIIB/C by context. Compare: Langada T10, Cos (Morricone 1967, 102, Fig. 82),
dating LHIIIC. Portes, Achaia (Ioannis Moschos pers. inf.).

TROY
No. 89 (Inventory no. 3250). Bronze dagger with "rat-tail". Well preserved. Triangular blade with pro-
nounced midrib. Brown to green patina.
L 38.6 cm. W 8.6 cm
Provenance: Troas. Bought in Athens 1887 (by Sophus Müller?).
Published: Undset 1890, 18, fig. 32. ESA X, 118, fig. 35b. Montelius. 1900, Fig. 383. Przeworski 1939 Pl.
18,2. Branigan 1974, 164, Cat. No. 483 (11). ("Short Swords"). Stronach 1957, Fig. 4, 3 (After Montelius
1900, Fig. 383).
Comments: DATING: Branigan 1974, 16: "… it is typologically closer to EBA spearhead types in the
Troad, the Cyclades and Anatolia generally". Stronach 1957: "… the Anatolian examples are all un-
stratified and can only be dated approximately by Cypriot models which are commonest between EC
Ib and EC IIa (cit. 106)". "EBI in Palestinian chronology or the beginning of the Early Bronze II – that
is: 3.200-2.750 BC" (Hestrin and Tadmor 1963, 28). DISTRIBUTION: The type is usual in Cyprus and
Anatolia (Stronach cit.) but also in Palestine (for instance from Kfar Monash, Hestrin and Tadmor 1963,
279-282).

No. 90 (Inventory no. 3248). Flat axe in bronze. Well preserved.
L 19.1 cm. Th 1.3 cm
Provenance: Troas. Bought from Rhousopoulos in Athens by Sophus Müller in April-May 1887 (stated
to be from Troas).
Published: ESA X, 118, Fig. 35a. Przeworski 1939, Tf. XVIII, 1. Branigan 1974, 166, no.595 (13).
("Flat-Axe Type I").
Comments: According to Branigan 1974, 24: Poliochni "Red". DATING: EB2. White Muscarella 1988,
410, nos. 552-561.

No. 91 (Inventory no. 3015). One half of a casting mould in steatite with two runners preserved. One end
not preserved. In one end are two symmetrically placed holes. On the back are a further two runners.
(mould for a spearhead?).
L 11, 2 cm. W 7, 3 cm. H 2, 8 cm. Width of groove 2, 8 cm. L of groove 9, 9 cm
Provenance: Hissarlik. Gift from Heinrich Schliemann 1885.
Unpublished
Comments: Schliemann Ilios p. 435, no. 105. DATING: Troy II-V/EBA (Schmidt 1902, 265).

CYPRUS

DAGGERS
No. 92 (Inventory no. 1077). Dagger of bronze. Well preserved with grey/brownish green patina. The
blade has slightly incurved edges, slightly raised mid rib and pointed shoulders. The blade continues from
the shoulders through a flat concave section into the flat tang with a rectangular section. A nail in the upper part of the tang is still preserved.
L 19.6 cm
Provenance: Lapithos Grave 314 A (9662-9686).

Unpublished
Comments: Stronach 1957 (Tp. 2). Catling 1964, fig. 3, 4 and p. 60. SCE I, p. 102, pl. xxvii, 3 (26). DATING: ECIII.

SPEARHEADS
No. 93 (Inventory no. 715). Spearhead of bronze. Well preserved with dark brown patina. Two opposed holes in the circular socket. Pointed oval blade tapering towards the point. Incised script sign on the blade near the socket.
L 22. 2 cm
Provenance: "Cyprus". Gift from Alexandria 1872.
Published: (ref. Congres international d'Anthropologie et d'Archeologie prehistorique 1869 (Cph. 1875), 482). Buchholz 1954, 133 ff. Ancient Cypriot Art 2001 (187) depicted on p. 96.
Comments: Compare Buchholz und Karageorghis 1971, 53 (no. 595) = Höckmann 1980, 27, Abb. 4 (D14), 134. DATING: LHIII (Höckmann cit.).

No. 94 (Inventory no. 714). Spearhead of bronze. Well preserved except for the edges of the blade. A bent nail is placed in a pierced hole in the circular socket where pieces of wood are still preserved. Long narrow blade with pronounced midrib.
L 32.5 cm
Provenance: "Cyprus". Gift from Alexandria 1872.
Published: (ref. Congres international d'Anthropologie et d'Archeologie prehistorique 1869 (Cph. 1875), 482). Ancient Cypriot Art 2001, p. 96 (no. 186) depicted on p. 96.
Comments: Richter 1915, nr. 1416. DATING: Late Cypriot.

No. 95 (Inventory no. 1074). Spearhead. Well preserved with grey/green patina. Long narrow pointed blade with rounded shoulders and pronounced mid rib. Solid tang with "rat-tail".
L 40.5 cm
Provenance: "Cyprus". Bought in Paris 1878.
Published: Ancient Cypriot Art 2001, 95 (no. 184), depicted on p. 95.
Comments: Compare SCE IV, 1a Fig. 98, 1-3 (ECIIIB). Catling 1964, pl. 12, f. DATING: ECIIIB.

No. 96 (Inventory no. 1076). Spearhead. Well preserved with black/green patina. Blade with curving edges, rounded butt, slightly marked midrib and rounded shoulders. The square tang ends in a "rat-tail".
L 20.0 cm
Provenance: "Cyprus". Bought in Paris 1878.
Published: Ancient Cypriot Art 2001, 93 (no. 182) depicted on p. 95.
Comments: Compare SCE IV, 1a, Fig. 97, 7. Stronach 1954, Fig. 4,1 (Tp. 1). DATING: ECI-III.

No. 97 (Inventory no. 1075). Spearhead (dagger?). Well preserved with brown, partly green patina. Narrow blade with almost straight edges, tapering towards the point. Rhomboid section (pronounced mid rib) and rounded shoulders. The mid rib continues in the tang which ends in a tap (point) with square section.
L 26. 2 cm
Provenance: "Cyprus". Bought in Paris 1878.
Published: Ancient Cypriot Art 2001, 93 (no. 181) depicted on p. 95.
Comments: Compare SCE IV, Fig. 98, 4 (?): DATING: ECIII.

FLAT AXES/CHISELS
No. 98 (Inventory no. 1073). Flat axe with out-curved edge and incurved sides. Well preserved with dark green patina.
L 14. 7 cm
Provenance: "Cyprus". Bought in Paris 1878.
Published: Ancient Cypriot Art 2001, 93 (no. 180), depicted on p. 94.

Comments: Richter 1915, no. 1620. Buchholz 1999, 488 (note 1903), Abb. 82, g (a piece from Ras Shamra). DATING: ECI-MCIII.

VARIOUS

No. 99 (Inventory no. 1032). A pair of tweezers. Rather damaged. Grey/brown patina.
L 9.3 cm
Provenance: "Cyprus". Bought in Paris 1878.
Published: Møller-Christensen 1938, p. 33, fig. 38. Ancient Cypriot Art 2001, p. 96 (no. 188) depicted on p. 96.
Comments: Richter 1915, no. 876. DATING: EBA.

No. 100 (Inventory no. 9686). Bronze arrowhead. The blade has rounded shoulders and tapers in a concave curve towards the rounded point. 'Slightly raised, wide midrib. Straight tang.
L 8. 5 cm
Provenance: Lapithos-Vrysi tou Barba, tomb. 314A. Gift from the Swedish Cyprus Expedition in 1935.
Published: SCE I, 102, pl. XXVII, 3 (26). Ancient Cypriot Art 2001, 95, Catalogue no. 185.
Comments: DATING: Late Cypriot.

No. 101 (Inventory no. 3547). A bull, bronze. The bull stands with slightly lowered head on straight legs apparently without any moulding of details. The ears protrude at right angles from the head.
L 8,15 cm. H (with horns) 5,5 cm
Provenance: Unknown. Bought 1890 in Paris (Feuardent) Kat. 21-22 marts 1890.
Published: Ancient Cypriot Art 2001, 93 (no. 178) fig. on p. 94.
Comments: Catling 1964, 249, no. 2, pl. 43, b-c. Caubet, Hermary and Karageorghis 1992, no. 59. DATING: LCIII.

No. 102 (Inventory no. 3538). Two pointed oval plates, bronze sheet ("Bronze blinkers"). Ovoid boss in the centre surrounded by a list. Two by two holes in the rim. (horse equipment?).
L 12. 7 cm. W 9. 1 cm
L 12, 1 cm. W 9. 4 cm
Provenance: "Cyprus". Bought in Paris 1890.
Published: Antiquités égyptiennes, phéniciennes, grecques et romaines. Vente ... à l'Hôtel Drouet 21-22.3. 1890 (no. 52). Ancient Cypriot Art 2001, 93 (no. 179). Drawings on p. 94.
Comments: DATING: Probably Iron Age.

No.103 (Inventory no. 9702). Arch fibula of bronze. The pin is broken and parts of the pin and sheath are missing.
L 5,5 cm
Provenance: Lapithos Grave 603. Gift from the Swedish Cyprus Expedition (Gjerstad) in 1935.
Published: SCE I, p. 274 ff. Pl. LVIII (9).
Comments: DATING: Cypro-geometric I (Blinkenberg 1926, 73, (Tp. II 17)).

THE NEAR EAST

SWORDS
No. 104 (Inventory no. 15645). Well-preserved sword of bronze. Tongue shaped blade with rhomboid section, pronounced mid rib and relief lines along the edges on both sides of the mid rib. The broad tang has rounded (convex) shoulders with one nail hole in each. The wide tang has flanged sides and two (still) preserved nails in the central line of the tang. The tang with "swallow tail" (shoulders) has a square point on the top.

L 65.4 cm. Max. W of tang (at shoulders). Max. W of blade: 3.3 cm
Provenance: According to the seller the piece was bought in Beirut in the 1950s (said by the seller to be probably from Cilicia). Bought by the National Museum in 1992.
Unpublished
Comments: Naue II Type. Comp. Catling 1956, 117 with reference to Riis 1948 (Hama) (Cowen 1955/56, Type Letten). DATING: 1.200-1.125 BC (Catling 1961, 120, Group III).

DAGGERS
No. 105 (Inventory no. 1113). Bronze dagger with flanged "wide tang". Brownish/reddish patina. The blade is rather corroded. Plastic rib dividing the blade from the broad tang.
L 20.5 cm
Provenance: "Unknown". From Løytved, Syria 1878.
Published: ESA X, 120, fig. 137. Riis 1957, 24. "Nihawand.type".
Comments: Iraq I, 1934, 163-168, Fig. 1. Schaeffer 1948, Pl. XIII, 4 from Ras Shamra. DATING: Ugarit Recent 2/RSI, 2 (1450-1365 BC).

No. 106 (Inventory no. 8979). Tongue shaped dagger (copper or bronze) with short broad tang and 4 nails, three in a line just above the transition between blade and tang. The point of the blade is broken.
L 24.0 cm
Provenance: Ur, Mesopotamia. Gift to the National Museum, received in 1929 from the British/American expedition to Ur (number written on the dagger U 10813A).
Unpublished
Comments: Zettler and Horne 1998, 169, no. 147/148. DATING: Early Dynastic III.

No. 107 (Inventory no. 8980). Dagger (bronze or copper?) with short broad tang. The flat blade with slightly pronounced midrib is pointed oval with one rounded and one angular shoulder. Part of organic material (wood?) found on the upper part of blade and lower part of the tang. One preserved nail in the centre of the lower part of the tang. Damage to the blade and bad corrosion.
L 18.3 cm
Provenance: Ur, Mesopotamia. Gift to the Museum. Received in 1929 from the British/American expedition to Ur.
Unpublished
Comments: DATING: Early Dynastic III.

No. 108 (Inventory no. 9904). Dagger with triangular haft. Dark green patina. Three nail holes in the haft placed in a triangular position. The flat blade without midrib is trapezoidal.
L 15.4 cm. W 3.5 cm
Provenance: Selemieh, Syria (30 km ESE of Hama). Gift to the museum in 1938.
Published: Dietz 1971, 12, fig. 7.
Comments: DATING: MBIIa (1.800-1750 BC) or slightly earlier.

SPEARHEADS
No. 109 (Inventory no. 1540). Bronze spearhead with tang. Badly corroded. The blade has a pronounced midrib and rounded shoulders, almost straight edges tapering towards the point. Incised ornaments on the upper part of the blade. The pointed tang is broader near the transition to the blade.
L 32.0 cm
Provenance: Syria. From Løytved 1881.
Unpublished
Comments: DATING: Compare no. 97 (Cyprus): EC III.

KNIVES

No. 110 (Inventory no. 8978). Fragment of a one edged bronze knife. Badly corroded. The tang is broken. The flat blade is broad; the edge is curved with an almost straight back.

L 13. 0 cm

Provenance: Ur. Gift to the National Museum. Received in 1929 from the British/American expedition to Ur.

Unpublished

Comments: ED III.

SOCKETED AXES

No. 111 (Inventory no. 3486). Shaft-hole axe. Slightly corroded. Circular shaft hole with collar and relief decoration on outside. The back is semicircular (in the shape of a cockscomb. The hanging edge is rounded. Dark green patina.

L 13.5 cm

Provenance: Syria. From Løytved, Beirut 1889/90.

Published: Archiv Orientalni VII 1935, 406, pl. 50 e. ESA X, 120. Przeworski 1939, Pl. 20, 5.

Comments: DATING: 2nd half of 2nd Mill. B.C. (Woolley 1936, 130 f. Fig. 3 (Tal Atchana)).

No. 112 (Inventory no. 14383). Shaft-hole axe. Light green patina. Straight-sided blade. The back is oblique. Depressed, curved areas around the circular shaft hole.

L 15.7 cm. Max. W 4.6 cm.

Provenance: According to the seller from Aleppo. Bought 1961.

Unpublished

No. 113 (Inventory no. 15033). Shaft-hole axe. Well preserved. Slightly oblique, circular shaft hole, with a heart-shaped upper opening. The lower edge of the socket is curved and extended downwards on the back-side. Behind the socket is a thick vertical plate with a horizontal bead just above the middle of the plate, cast integral with the socket. The blade is slim with an almost square section and vertical edge. Decorated with three horizontal relief bands at the upper part of the socket and three bands around the curved lower part of the socket.

L 18.4 cm. H 8.0 cm

Provenance: Not stated. Bought 1969.

Unpublished

Comments: Compare Tell Ahmar – til Barsib (Syria) (Tombe -Hypogée), Schaeffer 1948, 81, Fig. 82, 22 (2.300 -2.000 BC). Luristan (2.300-2.100 BC), Schaeffer 1948, Fig. 263, 3 (said to be a sumerian type).

No. 114 (Inventory no. 14965). Shaft-hole axe of bronze. Well preserved. Green/black patina. "Pelta shaped" blade with an oval shaft hole. On the reverse side of the axe two extensions are seen creating a support for the shaft. At the back-side of the axe between the two extensions, a drop-shaped knob is placed. The semicircular edge terminates in grooves where the shaft is supported. Decorative lists are placed along the inner openings.

W (from edge to knob) 11.1 cm. L edge: 9.9 cm. Shaft-hole dimensions: 2.0 × 2.6 cm

Provenance: Unknown.

Unpublished

Comments: "The type is of Syrian origin, but also known from the Middle Kingdom in Egypt (XII dyn.)". Flinders Petrie 1917, 10, Pl. LXXIV, 171. Also Flinders Petrie 1925). DATING: XII dynasty.

BRONZE RINGS

No. 115 (Inventory no. 3473). Spiral ring of bronze. Well preserved. Green/black patina. Terminating in animal heads. Inside flat, outside curved.

D 9,2 cm

Provenance: Lebanon. From Løytved 1889.
Unpublished

VARIOUS
No. 116 (Inventory no. 8982). Pin. At the end a "tap". The section is octagonal. A hole is pierced through the pin in the upper end. From a fibula (?)
L 16.4 cm
Provenance: Ur (U 8262). Gift from the British/American expedition to Ur 1929.
Unpublished
Comments: DATING: ED III.

BRONZE FIGURINES
No. 117 (Inventory no. 1522). Standing nude female figurine. There is a ribbon around the head and its ends are indicated at the nape. The top of the head inside the ribbon is flat. The features of the face are not well executed, the nose is rather dominant. The arms are crossed in front of the chest, the breasts shaped like small knobs. The feet are broken off. Brownish patina.
H. 5,4 cm
Provenance: Not indicated. Gift to the National Museum from Julius Løytved in 1880/81.
Published: ESA X, 121. Buhl 1977, 139.
Comments: In ESA X described as a male figurine. Buhl 1977 probably rightly considered it to be a female figurine. A male parallel in the British Museum was found in Syria (Negbi 1968, 47, fig. 2, no.8) and dated, based on pieces from Hama (Buhl 1977, 139-140, Fig. p. 142) around 1800 B.C. Pieces from a hoard in Tall al Judaidah (phases G to H, first centuries of the 3rd Mill) are considered prototypes for the "divine couple" (Braidwood 1960, 300 ff, Pls. 57 – 64 and Buhl 1977, 140). DATING: Around 1.800 B.C.

No. 118 (Inventory no. 1536). Badly-corroded bronze figurine of a standing, naked woman with wavy hair in front and long hair (pig-tail) down the back to the waist. The breasts are well developed, the arms are reaching forwards. Below the feet a tenon. Lower part of the right arm is missing. Brownish patina.
H 8.6 cm
Provenance: Byblos. Bought by Deputy Consul Løytved in Syria 1881.
Published: ESA X, 121. Buhl 1977, 144 (no. 12), depicted on p. 149.
Commments: Parallel from Byblos (Dunand 1954 (text), 131, no. 7638 and Pl. CLXIV)(Dunand 1950) (dated by Dunand to the Hyksos Period). As for comparison with ivory of Syro-Hittite origin, see especially Barnett 1975, 128, Pl. CXXII, no. V 16 and Barnett 1936, 121-123. DATING: Last quarter of 2nd Mill. B.C. (after Barnett).

No. 119 (Inventory no. 1989). Bronze figurine depicting a naked woman with the right-hand forefinger on the mouth and the left hand on the back. The figure terminates in a tang.
H 11.5 cm
Provenance: Bought in Beirut from Deputy Consul Løytved in 1882.
Published: ESA X, 121.

No. 120 (Inventory no. 1990). Human figurine in bronze. On the head a pointed cap seems indicated. The eyes are shaped as circular buttons. A beard is perhaps indicated. The figure is depicted walking with both hands outstretched. Tang below the feet. Brownish patina.
H 8.5 cm
Provenance: Unknown. Syria (?) Acquired from Løytved 1882.
Published: ESA X, 121. Buhl 1977, 140 (no. 4), depicted on p. 143.
Comments: Compare Byblos "Temple aux Obélisques" (Dunand 1950, Pl. 110, no. 15482 and another one without context in Dunand 11958, 910, fig. 1021, no. 17275). Also Dunand 1958, Pl. CX (1548), "Temple aux Obelisques Depot d'offrandes de la …" (15121-15566). DATING: 19th to 18th century B.C.

No. 121 (Inventory no. 1991). Small figurine in bronze depicting a standing wild goat. Standing on a plate with five holes. A lug on the back. A decoration with "Eyes" and dots is indicated by incised and drilled circles. Brown black patina.

H 4.0 cm

Provenance: unknown. Bought from Deputy Consul Løytved in Beirut.

Published: Buhl 1977, 152, no. 16. ESA X, 119.

Comments: DATING: 8th century B.C. (Buhl 1977, 152).

No. 122 (Inventory no. 5037). Bronze figurine depicting a standing man with a conical cap on his head. The lower part of the body is wrapped in a kilt. The arms are kept together in front of the person. In the right hand he holds a small goblet. Below each foot there is a tenon. Black patina.

H 11.7 cm

Provenance: Lebanon. Deposited in the National Museum after the death of Julius Løytved in 1912.

Published: Buhl 1977, 142 (no. 6), depicted on p. 145 (ref. Clermont-Ganneau, Album d'antiquites orientales pl. 49, 4). ESA X, 121.

Comments: Influenced by Egyptian prototypes. Collon 1972, passim and the "Smiting God Types" kept in the Jar 2000 in Byblos (Dunand 1937, pl. 58, no. 2031). DATING: After 1900 BC.

No. 123 (Inventory no. 5155). Female figurine in bronze. The woman is standing with the lower part of her body covered by a narrow shirt, close-fitting on the lower part, folded on the upper. On the front are two hanging textile folds. The upper part of the body is naked. The hands are holding the breasts. Left ear is pierced. No patina.

H 11.6 cm

Provenance: Asia Minor. Bought in London 1902.

Published: ESA X, 119.

No. 124 (Inventory no. 7032). Babylonian bronze figure bearing a basket. No inscriptions visible! Badly-corroded surface. A tenon below the feet.

H 24,8 cm

Provenance: From around Mosul. Bought in London (received at the National Museum in 1913).

Unpublished

Comments: So called "foundation figurine" comp. Rashid 1983, no 114 (Gudea) (from Tello). (ref. Sarzec de Heuzey: Decouvertes en Chaldee 1884-1912, pl. 28, no. 2 (CIVI). Sarzec de Heuzey 1902, no. 158). Ellis 1968, 61, Fig. 19. DATING: New Sumerian (Late 3rd Mill.)(Rashid 1983).

No. 125 (Inventory no. 7319). Bronze figure from the so-called Smiting God Group. High conical cap on the head. The right arm is raised and the left arm stretched forward. Both hands are clenched in order to hold objects which are now missing. The figure wears a short kilt with a belt. The left leg is placed in front of the right. Below each foot there is a tenon. Slices for fixing gold and silver coating on the rear part of the cap, on the lower part of both arms, along the sides up to the end of the skirt and along the rear of the legs. Greenish-black patina.

H 15.5 cm

Provenance: No provenance indicated. Acquired from an antique dealer (Joseph Altounian) in Paris, 1920.

Published: ESA. X, 120 Fig. 38. Associazione Internationale di Studi Mediterranei 2, Bulletino Aprile-Maggio 1931, 1, Pl. 3, no. 4. Buhl 1977, 144 (no. 10), depicted p. 148.

Compare: As for the Smiting God Group in general see Collon 1972. DATING: Closest parallel from Megiddo levels IX-VII (1550-1150 BC). (Collon 1972, 115, fig. 2, no. 17. Loud 1948, pl. 235, no. 22). Figurines from Ras Shamra/Minat al Baida indicates a more specific dating of the type to first half of the 14th century BC (Collon 1972, 128 f.).

No. 126 (Inventory no. 3357). Number left out!

No. 127 (Inventory no. 7320). Figure in bronze of a naked man with a conical cap (helmet). Large triangular head. The large ears are pierced for earrings. The lower arms are bent at the elbows and stretched forward in a horizontal position. The figure is placed on the left leg with the right turned back (the right leg probably bent in modern times). A hole is pierced through the hips. Brown, partly grey/greenish patina. H 11.2 cm

Provenance: Syria. Purchased in Paris 1920 from the dealer Joseph Altounian.

Published: ESA X 121. Buhl 1977, 140 (no. 5) depicted p. 145.

Comments: From Byblos (Parrot et al. 1975, fig. 24 and Dunand 1958, pl. 170, no. 11241 (terracotta figurine depicting herdsmen leading their oxen)). DATING: Beginning of the 2nd Mill. B.C. (For further references see Buhl 1977, 141-142).

No. 128 (Inventory no. 13811). Male figure in bronze, perhaps depicting the Syrian God Haddad. The triangular face has a pointed chin (a beard?), small mouth, protruding nose and deep eye-sockets. The muscles on the upper arms are prominent, the lower arms are stretched forward. The nipples are clearly indicated. A torque is placed around the long neck. Short kilt with a belt in which a dagger pommel appears. The lower part of the weapon protrudes below the kilt. The head bears a feather crown which could be an imitation of the Egyptian double crown or a feather crown with the Uraeus snake. The crude feet, the left a little in front of the right, stand on a base with a long stem ending in a tenon that has preserved the shape of the casting channel. Reddish/brown patina.
H 15.0 cm

Provenance: Unknown. Bought in Rome 1957.

Published: Buhl 1977, 143 (no. 9), depicted p. 147.

Comments: Compare a similar piece found in Tall Simriyan (Braidwood 1940, 212, pl. 26). Grasped in the right hand of the Simriyan statuette was an axe, no doubt a "window-axe". In the right hand was a thunderbolt. Another parallel is from Ras Shamra (Schaeffer 1949, 73, Fig. 31). Our figure is considered to be the male half of a divine couple and is included in a group of bronzes named after Simriyan (Negbi 1961, 114 fig. 5. Porada 1942, 58-59). DATING: In Simriyan the piece was included in the Middle Bronze levels (Braidwood 1940). Negbi considered the group to have been produced within the MB II A-B periods (Albright). Schaeffer 1949, Ugarit Moyen 1/Ugarit Moyen 2 (2000-1800 B.C.).

No. 129 (Inventory no. 7296). Hittite bronze figurine. A god is standing on the back of a bull; man and bull are cast in one piece. The man wears a high pointed cap, and has a broad beard under the cheek. His left hand is placed on his chest, his right is outstretched. Damage to the left horn, left front leg and right hind leg.
H 6.0 cm

Provenance: Djerabulous (Karkemish). Bought from Dr.med. E. Løytved (son of the deputy consul) who found it himself in Djerabulus.

Published: Buhl 1977, 150-51 (n.15) depicted on p. 151. Przeworski 1936, 35, pl. IX. ESA X, 121. Przeworski 1939, Pl. 14, 5. Ref. also Braidwood 1940, 63. Bossert 1942, 144, fig. 610. Dunand 1956, Pl. LXI. "Champ des offrandes ..."

Comments: DATING: Middle of the 13th century B.C.

No. 130 (Inventory no. 15090). Statue of bronze of an offering bearer. Breasts, strongly emphasized, and navel are indicated under the long garment. On the head is a piece of conical headgear in Egyptian style with an ostrich feather on each side (the so-called Atef crown without the ram's horns). The left arm stretches forward bearing a bowl. The right arm has likewise been stretched forward but is broken above the elbow. The feet are held together with a tenon below. Brownish patina.

H (+tang) 13.8 cm. H (- tang) 11.5 cm

Provenance: Unknown. Acquired in 1972.

Published: Buhl 1977, 144 (no. 11), depicted p. 149.

Comments: DATING: The figurine should be compared to a seated god in Minat al Baida representing a seated Phoenician god dated to the 14th cent. BC (Schaeffer 1936, Pl. XV, 3).

No. 131 (Inventory no. 15200). Statuette of bronze. Person sitting with a long coat, with sleeves or a short mantle. The coat has a thick border at the lower termination. The feet are together Below the feet, a tenon. The left arm of the figure is placed on the left leg; the right arm with the hand has a clenched fist placed on the right knee. The face is worn, the ears are well preserved. On top of the head a crown with concave sides and rounded top. A hole in the back and under the seat up to the waist.
H 7.6 cm
Provenance: Unknown.
Unpublished
Comments: North Syrian type.

No. 132 (Inventory no. 13366). Bridle ring of copper (?) with a wild donkey (onager or wild ass) on an oval plate on top of the circular rings (for the bridles), placed on a vertical tenon. The tenon terminates in a hoop (plate) with two dowels. Dark brown to greenish patina.
H 19.5 cm. W (max.) 9.5 cm
Provenance: Nasiriyah. Gift from the Ny Carlsberg Foundation 1953.
Published: Riis 1957, 22. Iraq X, 1948. A copper/ring from Southern Iraq.
Comments: DATING: Mallowan 1948, 51-55, Pls. VII-VIII): "end of 2nd or the beginning of the 3rd Early Dynastic period, ca. 2.500 BC". Zettler and Horne 1998, 165, Fig. 52 from Ur (Woolley 1934, Pl. 166 (U.10439).

BOWLS
No. 133 (Inventory no. 8977). Bowl in bronze. Badly corroded.
H 6,0 cm. D 12.0 cm
Provenance: Ur (U 9073?). Gift from the British/American expedition to Ur, 1929.
Unpublished
Comments: DATING: ED III.

No. 134 (Inventory no. 8976). Silver bowl. Fragmented. Flat bottom. In the wall a boss with traces of bronze preserved.
D 14.7 cm
Provenance: Ur (U 10918). Gift from the British/American expedition to Ur 1929.
Unpublished
Comments: DATING: ED III.

No. 135 (Inventory no. 15094). Shaft-hole axe ("window axe"/"duck-bill axe"), silver. Well preserved. Preserved on one side is an inlay of silver/electrum granulation in a raised zone at right angles to the edge. On the other side two small grooves are seen where a similar inlay had been placed. The shaft hole is flattened at the ends. A few pieces are missing.
L 12.9 cm. W 8.3 cm
Provenance: Unknown. Bought 1972
Unpublished
Comments: Very usual Near Eastern type. Comp. Dunand 1958, 133-135 (axes in gold) from "Temple aux obelisques. Depot d'offrandes". Buchholz 1999, 608 (and note 2350), Abb. 100, b-c (and the relations with Crete). DATING: Ras Shamra-Ugarit (Syria) dated to Ugarit Moyen (2.100-1.900 BC)(According to Schaeffer 1948, Fig. 56).

BOAT
No. 136 (Inventory no. 7071). Votive boat in silver. Slightly damaged.
L 31.0 cm. W 4.5 cm.
H (max.) 9.0 cm.
Provenance: Warka (around Baghdad). Bought in Paris 1913.
Published: Salonen 1939. 43 (note 1), 157, Pl. X, 1. Louisiana Revy nr. 3, 18. aarg. 1978. Kat. Nr. 33, p. 36.

APPENDIX (by Lasse Sørensen)

A NOTE ON SOME MYCENAEAN GOLD OBJECTS, OBSIDIAN AND FLINT ARROWHEADS bought in 1904 by Christian Blinkenberg from Drakopoulos in Athens. The dealer stated that the objects had been purchased from "the heirs of a peasant who had worked for Schliemann".

FLINT AND OBSIDIAN
Lasse Sørensen

INTRODUCTION
The collection consists of 24 leaf-shaped arrowheads. All the arrowheads have been dated to the LH I phase and have been classified as a Type IVa, consistent with the typological studies of Buchholz (1962, 11). The arrowheads of this particular type are characterised by having a u-shaped base.
The article by Buchholz is so far the most detailed research into the lithic arrowheads from the prehistoric Aegean. In general the research into lithic arrowheads in the Aegean is very limited, and no recent systematic study of the arrowheads has yet been conducted. This lack of interest in the Mycenaean lithic technology is remarkable, mainly because the information concerning the arrowheads context is often readily available and thus contains a vast amount of research potential. The arrowheads are often not illustrated and tend to be described as "found in large numbers" or "coarsely or primitive worked" (Schliemann 1886, 43), although many of these arrowheads are actually masterpieces in terms of flint technology (Buchholz 1962, 24).

The information about this particular arrowhead collection is scarce. According to the records at the Danish National Museum, Christian Blinkenberg bought these arrowheads together with several gold objects (5655-5665) in 1904 from an antique dealer in Athens. It was stated by the dealer, that the pieces derived from the heirs of a peasant who had worked for Schliemann. The same types of gold objects and arrowheads have been found in the Mycenae Shaft Graves (Schliemann 1878; Karo 1930). It is thus possible, that the arrowheads may be linked to the Mycenae Shaft Grave complex. Schliemann mentions the arrowheads from Shaft Grave IV (Schliemann 1878, 311ff) and stone arrowheads found in Mycenae or Tiryns (Schliemann 1886, 162). He does not give many indications of the exact context of these pieces. The 24 arrowheads from our collection might thus have originated in either Mycenae or Tiryns.

The majority of the 24 points are made of Melian obsidian (5628-5647), some are of honey flint (5648-5649) and light greyish flint (5650-5651). Most arrowheads from the Late Helladic were made out of obsidian and radiolarite (Buchholz 1962, 21; Druart 2006). The points made of obsidian and honey flint indicate that Mycenaean society had access to raw materials of a high quality (Parkinson 1999, 84). The arrowheads have all been produced by parallel pressure percussion. The pressure percussion is applied with the narrow end of a tool made of wood, antler, bone or metal. The bifacial shaping of the arrowheads started with a flake, as can be observed on arrowhead 5649. The points are generally finely pressured on both faces and display thin biconvex cross-sections. In the final production stage, the points were finished by carving the u-shaped base of the arrowheads. This particular technique was used to control the shaping of the point (Evely 1993, 137ff; Inizan et al. 1999, 31ff). The technique creates some very characteristic arrowheads, which are very thin with thickness varying from 1-to 3 mm. The width of these arrowheads is rather canonical and tends to be around 1 cm. Many of the points were fragmented (5631-5647 and 5650-5651) and only a few of the arrowheads (5628, 5629, 5630, 5648 and 5649) were complete. The fracture is caused by either the result of use as a projectile point or accidental breaks (Fischer et al. 1984, 19ff). The macroscopic features on the projectile points are dominated by a snap terminating bending fracture (5631-5635, 5638-5639, 5640-5642, 5644-5646 and 5650). Some of the arrowheads also had a step terminating bending fracture (5636, 5643, 5647 and 5651). Especially the last type of fracture suggests, that these arrowheads may indeed have been used for warfare or hunting purposes during Late Helladic times (Fischer et al. 1984, 23f).

The Production of the lithic arrowheads concentrated on the Aegean Mainland, where specialized flint-knappers were employed (Buchholz 1962, 28; Dickinson 1994, 198; Kardulias 1999, 69ff). Especially arrowheads of Type IVa is found in Mycenean grave complexes in the Peloponnese, Attica and Boeotia during the Late Helladic I – III periods. According to Buchholz (1962, 36ff), Type IVa arrowheads have been found in many chamber-, dome-, and tholos graves at: Volimidia (Buchholz 1962, 37. Pic. 9b, 9d & 10t), Kakovatos grave A (Buchholz 1962, 37. Pic. 9c, 9f, 9j, 9l & 9u), Malthi (Buchholz 1962, 37. Pic. 9p, 9t & 10m), Kynouria (Buchholz 1962, 38. Pic. 9a, 9e & 9r), Dendra Grave 8 and 515 (Buchholz 1962, 38f. Pic. 9h, 9m, 9o, 10a, 10f, 10o & 10δ), Prosymna Grave 2, 14, 26, 34, 44 & 49 (Buchholz 1962, 38ff. Pic. 9v, 9x, 9y, 10b, 10e, 10g, 10n, 10u, 10x, 10y, 10z, 10α & 10ζ), Goubalari Grave I and II (Buchholz 1962, 41. Pic. 10c, 10d, 10h, 10i & 10k), Asine (Buchholz 1962, 42. Pic. 10v), Palast (Buchholz 1962, 40. Pic. 9g), Theben (Buchholz 1962, 40. Pic. 9i & 9q), Eutresis (Buchholz 1962, 40. Pic. 9w & 9α) and the Mycenae Shaft Grave IV (Buchholz 1962, 39. Pic. 9n, 9z, 9γ-9η). Finally, a rare example of a Type IVa arrowhead has been observed at Knossos (Buchholz 1962, 36).

These types of arrowheads can thus be associated with graves linked to the Mycenaean male elites. The numerous arrowheads from Late Helladic graves indicate that the bow was a standard Mycenaean weapon, which was closely linked to such activities as hunting or warfare (Buchholz 1962, 28f; Hamilakis 2003, 243f). It can also be observed in the Mycenaean iconography, where hunting scenes are among the most popular themes. The Mycenaean elite continued to use these masterpieces of lithic arrowheads into the Late Helladic III, until they were gradually replaced by points made of bronze.

CATALOGUE

Inventory no. 5628. Leaf-shaped arrowhead of obsidian. The arrowhead is a Type IVa according to the Buchholz typology (1962, 11). Technique: Parallel pressure percussion with parallel retouches.
L 2.25 cm. W 1.00 cm. T 0.22 cm
Provenance: Bought from an antique dealer in Athens in 1904. Purchased from the heirs of a peasant who had worked for Schliemann.
Comments: DATING: LHI.

Inventory no. 5629. Leaf-shaped arrowhead of obsidian. The arrowhead is a Type IVa according to the Buchholz typology (1962, 11). Technique: Parallel pressure percussion with parallel retouches.
L 2.25 cm. W 1.1 cm. T 0.2 cm
Provenance: As no. 5628.
Comments: DATING: LHI.

Inventory no. 5630. Leaf-shaped arrowhead of obsidian. The arrowhead is a Type IVa according to the Buchholz typology (1962, 11). Technique: Parallel pressure percussion with parallel retouches.
L 3.65 cm. W 1.05 cm. T 0.2 cm.
Provenance: As no. 5628.
Comments: DATING: LHI.

Inventory no. 5631. Leaf-shaped arrowhead of obsidian, with a snap terminating bending fracture on the tip of the point (Fischer et al. 1984, 23). The arrowhead is a Type IVa according to the Buchholz typology (1962, 11). Technique: Parallel pressure percussion with parallel retouches.
L 3 cm. W 1.3 cm. T 0.2 cm.
Provenance: As no. 5628.
Comments: DATING: LHI.

Inventory no. 5632. Leaf-shaped arrowhead of obsidian, with a snap terminating bending fracture on the tip of the point (Fischer et al. 1984, 23). The arrowhead is a Type IVa according to the Buchholz typology (1962, 11). Technique: Parallel pressure percussion with parallel retouches.
L 3 cm. W 1.1 cm. T 0.15 cm.
Provenance: As no. 5628.
Comments: DATING: LHI.

Inventory no. 5633. Leaf-shaped arrowhead of obsidian, with a snap terminating bending fracture on the tip of the point and a fragmented base (Fischer et al. 1984, 23). The arrowhead is a Type IVa according to the Buchholz typology (1962, 11). Technique: Parallel pressure percussion with parallel retouches.
L 2.4 cm. W 1.1 cm. T 0.15 cm.
Provenance: As no. 5628.
Comments: DATING: LHI.

Inventory no. 5634. Leaf-shaped arrowhead of obsidian, with a snap terminating bending fracture on the tip of the point (Fischer et al. 1984, 23). The arrowhead is a Type IVa according to the Buchholz typology (1962, 11). Technique: Parallel pressure percussion with parallel retouches.
L 2.4 cm. W 1 cm. T 0.13 cm.
Provenance: As no. 5628.
Comments: DATING: LHI.

Inventory no. 5635. Leaf-shaped arrowhead of obsidian, with a snap terminating bending fracture on the tip of the point and a fragmented base (Fischer et al. 1984, 23). The arrowhead is a Type IVa according to the Buchholz typology (1962, 11). Technique: Parallel pressure percussion with parallel retouches.
L 2.2 cm. W 0.9 cm. T 0.12 cm.
Provenance: As no. 5628.
Comments: DATING: LHI.

Inventory no. 5636. Leaf-shaped arrowhead of obsidian, with a step terminating bending fracture on the tip of the point and a fragmented base (Fischer et al. 1984, 23). The arrowhead is a Type IVa according to the Buchholz typology (1962, 11). Technique: Parallel pressure percussion with parallel retouches.
L 2.15 cm. W 1.03 cm. T 0.15 cm.
Provenance: As no. 5628.
Comments: DATING: LHI.

Inventory no. 5637. Leaf-shaped arrowhead of obsidian, with a fragmented base. The arrowhead is a Type IVa according to the Buchholz typology (1962, 11). Technique: Parallel pressure percussion with parallel retouches.
L 2.45 cm. W 1 cm. T 0.15 cm.
Provenance: As no. 5628.
Comments: DATING: LHI.

Inventory no. 5638. Leaf-shaped arrowhead of obsidian, with a snap terminating bending fracture on the tip of the point (Fischer et al. 1984, 23). The arrowhead is a Type IVa according to the Buchholz typology (1962, 11). Technique: Parallel pressure percussion with parallel retouches.
L 2.1 cm. W 0.9 cm. T 0.12 cm
Provenance:As no. 5628.
Comments: DATING: LHI.

Inventory no. 5639. Leaf-shaped arrowhead of obsidian, with a snap terminating bending fracture on the tip of the point (Fischer et al. 1984, 23). The arrowhead is a Type IVa according to the Buchholz typology (1962, 11). Technique: Parallel pressure percussion with parallel retouches.

L 1.7 cm. W 1 cm. T 0.23 cm.
Provenance: As no. 5628.
Comments: DATING: LHI.

Inventory no. 5640. Leaf-shaped arrowhead of obsidian, with a snap terminating bending fracture on the tip of the point (Fischer et al. 1984, 23). The arrowhead is a Type IVa according to the Buchholz typology (1962, 11). Technique: Parallel pressure percussion with parallel retouches.
L 2.7 cm. W 1.2 cm. T 0.18 cm
Provenance:As no. 5628.
Comments: DATING: LHI.

Inventory no. 5641. Leaf-shaped arrowhead of obsidian, with a snap terminating bending fracture on the tip of the point (Fischer et al. 1984, 23). The arrowhead is a Type IVa according to the Buchholz typology (1962, 11). Technique: Parallel pressure percussion with parallel retouches.
L 2.55 cm. W 1.0 cm. T 0.2 cm
Provenance:As no. 5628.
Comments: DATING: LHI.

Inventory no. 5642. Leaf-shaped arrowhead of obsidian, with a snap terminating bending fracture on the tip of the point and a fragmented base (Fischer et al. 1984, 23). The arrowhead is a Type IVa according to the Buchholz typology (1962, 11). Technique: Parallel pressure percussion with parallel retouches.
L 2.7 cm. W 1.05 cm. T 0.2 cm.
Provenance: As no. 5628.
Comments: DATING: LHI.

Inventory no. 5643. Leaf-shaped arrowhead of obsidian, with a step terminating bending fracture on the tip of the point (Fischer et al. 1984, 23). The arrowhead is a Type IVa according to the Buchholz typology (1962, 11). Technique: Parallel pressure percussion with parallel retouches.
L 2 cm. W 1.1 cm. T 0.2 cm.
Provenance: As no. 5628.
Comments: DATING: LHI.

Inventory no. 5644. Leaf-shaped arrowhead of obsidian, with a snap terminating bending fracture on the tip of the point (Fischer et al. 1984, 23). The arrowhead is a Type IVa according to the Buchholz typology (1962, 11). Technique: Parallel pressure percussion with parallel retouches.
L 2.35 cm. W 1.05 cm. T 0.15 cm
Provenance: As no. 5628.
Comments: DATING: LHI.

Inventory no. 5645. Leaf-shaped arrowhead of obsidian, with a snap terminating bending fracture on the tip of the point and a fragmented base (Fischer et al. 1984, 23). The arrowhead is a Type IVa according to the Buchholz typology (1962, 11). Technique: Parallel pressure percussion with parallel retouches.
L. 2.2 cm. W. 0.9 cm. T. 0.2 cm.
Provenance: As no. 5628.
Comments: DATING: LHI.

Inventory no. 5646. Leaf-shaped arrowhead of obsidian, with a snap terminating bending fracture on the tip of the point (Fischer et al. 1984, 23). The arrowhead is a Type IVa according to the Buchholz typology (1962, 11). Technique: Parallel pressure percussion with parallel retouches.
L. 2.1 cm. W. 1 cm. T. 0.12 cm.
Provenance: As no. 5628.
Comments: DATING: LHI.

Inventory no. 5647. Leaf-shaped arrowhead of obsidian, with a step terminating bending fracture on the tip of the point and a fragmented base (Fischer et al. 1984, 23). The arrowhead is a Type IVa according to the Buchholz typology (1962, 11). Technique: Parallel pressure percussion with parallel retouches.
L. 2.15 cm. W. 1.1 cm. T. 0.15 cm.
Provenance: As no. 5628.
Comments: DATING: LHI.

Inventory no. 5648. Leafshaped arrowhead of honey flint. The arrowhead is a Type IVa according to the Buchholz typology (1962, 11). Technique: Parallel pressure percussion with parallel retouches.
L. 4 cm. W. 1.35 cm. T. 0.25 cm.
Provenance: As no. 5628.
Comments: DATING: LHI.

Inventory no. 5649. Leaf-shaped arrowhead of honey flint. The arrowhead is a Type IVa according to the Buchholz typology (1962, 11). Technique: Parallel pressure percussion with parallel retouches.
L. 3.2 cm. W. 1.2 cm. T. 0.2 cm.
Provenance: As no. 5628.
Comments: DATING: LHI.

Inventory no. 5650. Leaf-shaped arrowhead of light greyish flint, with a snap terminating bending fracture on the tip of the point (Fischer et al. 1984, 23). The arrowhead is a Type IVa according to the Buchholz typology (1962, 11). Technique: Parallel pressure percussion with parallel retouches.
L 2 cm. W 1.15 cm. T 0.15 cm.
Provenance: As no. 5628.
Comments: DATING: LHI.

Inventory no. 5651. Leaf-shaped arrowhead of light greyish flint, with a step terminating bending fracture on the tip of the point and a fragmented base (Fischer et al. 1984, 23). The arrowhead is a Type IVa according to the Buchholz typology (1962, 11). Technique: Parallel pressure percussion with parallel retouches.
L. 2 cm. W. 1.2 cm. T. 0.2 cm
Provenance: As no. 5628.
Comments: DATING: LHI.

CATALOGUE OF GOLD AND BONE OBJECTS
Inventory no. 5652. Convex disc of thin gold foil with folded edges. Slightly damaged. Incised decorations with meander band around dots.
D. 3.4 cm
Provenance: Bought from an antique dealer in Athens in 1904. Purchased from the heirs of a peasant who had worked for Schliemann.
Unpublished
Comments: Karo 1930-33, Pl. LX, no. 334 (Grave IV) and Pl. LXIII, no. 675 (Grave V). DATING: LHI.

Inventory no. 5653. Convex disc of thin gold foil with folded edges. Slightly damaged. Incised decoration with circles around centre marked with a dot, framed by a circle produced by three concentric circles near the rim.
D. 2.2 cm
Provenance: As no. 5652.
Comments: Karo 1930-33, Pl. LX, no. 321 (Grave IV) and Pl. LXII, no. 680 (?) (Grave V). DATING: LHI.

Inventory no. 5654. Convex disc of thin gold foil with folded edges. Decorated with incised concentric circles.
D. 2.2 cm
Provenance: As no. 5652.
Unpublished
Comments: Karo 1930-33, no. 314, Pl. LIX (Grave IV) and no. 667, Pl. LXII (Grave V). DATING: LHI.

Inventory no. 5655. Convex disc of thin gold foil with folded edges. Decorated with incised concentric circles.
D. 2.2 cm
Provenance: As no. 5652.
Unpublished
Comments: Karo 1930-33, no. 314, Pl. LIX (Grave IV) and no. 667, Pl. LXII (Grave V). DATING: LHI.

Inventory no. 5656. Convex disc of thin gold foil with folded edges. Decorated with incised concentric circles.
D. 1.6 cm
Provenance: As no. 5652.
Unpublished
Comments: Karo 1930-33, no. 314, Pl. LIX (Grave IV) and no. 667, Pl. LXII (Grave V). DATING: LHI.

Inventory no. 5657. Convex disc of thin gold foil with folded edges. Decorated with incised concentric circles.
D. 1.6 cm
Provenance: As no. 5652.
Unpublished
Comments: Karo 1930-33, no. 314, Pl. LIX (Grave IV) and no. 667, Pl. LXII (Grave V). DATING: LHI.

Inventory no. 5658. Convex disc of thin gold foil with folded edges. Decorated with incised concentric circles.
D. 1.2 cm
Provenance: As no. 5652.
Unpublished
Comments: Karo 1930-33, no. 314, Pl. LIX (Grave IV) and no. 667, Pl. LXII (Grave V). DATING: LHI.

Inventory no. 5659. Convex disc of thin gold foil with folded edges. Entirely preserved but somewhat damaged.
D. 1.2 cm
Provenance: As no. 5652.
Unpublished
Comments: Karo 1930-33. DATING: LHI.

Inventory no. 5660. Convex disc of thin gold foil with folded edges. Entirely preserved but somewhat damaged.
D. 1.0 cm
Provenance: As no. 5652.
Unpublished
Comments: Karo 1930-33. DATING: LHI.

Inventory no. 5661 Circular, disc shaped button with three incised concentric circles in the centre (probably covered with gold-foil).
Unpublished
Provenance: As no. 5652.

Inventory no. 5662. Four cylindrical gold beads. Made from short tubes with four rows of round gold beads.
L. 0.6-0.7 cm
Provenance: As no. 5652.
Comments: DATING: LHI.

Inventory no. 5664. Four pieces of gold foil without decoration.
L. 2.3-4.6 cm. W. 1.0 cm
Provenance: As no. 5652.
Comments: DATING: LHI.

Inventory no. 5665. Gold nail with convex head.
L. 0.9 cm
Provenance: As no. 5652.
Comments: Karo 1930-33, Pl. CXLVI, nos. 803-806 (Grave V). DATING: LHI.

Inventory no. 5666. Six pieces of bone.
Provenance: As no. 5652.
Measurements missing
Comments: The longer bone sticks (a-b) have incised circle-decoration with concentric circles with marked centre – 12 (b and d), 13 (a) or 14 (c). The meaning of the circle decoration is unclear (game/counting). All six could used as tools for parallel pressure percussion of obsidian or flint (arrowheads). DATING: LHI.

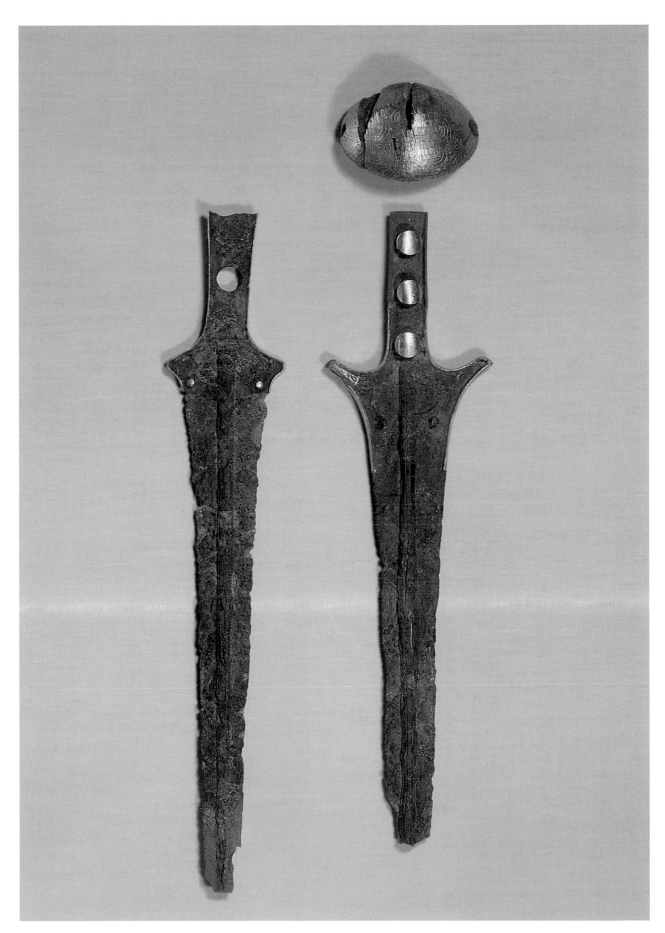

Fig. 1

Fig. 2

Plate I

THE AEGEAN AREA

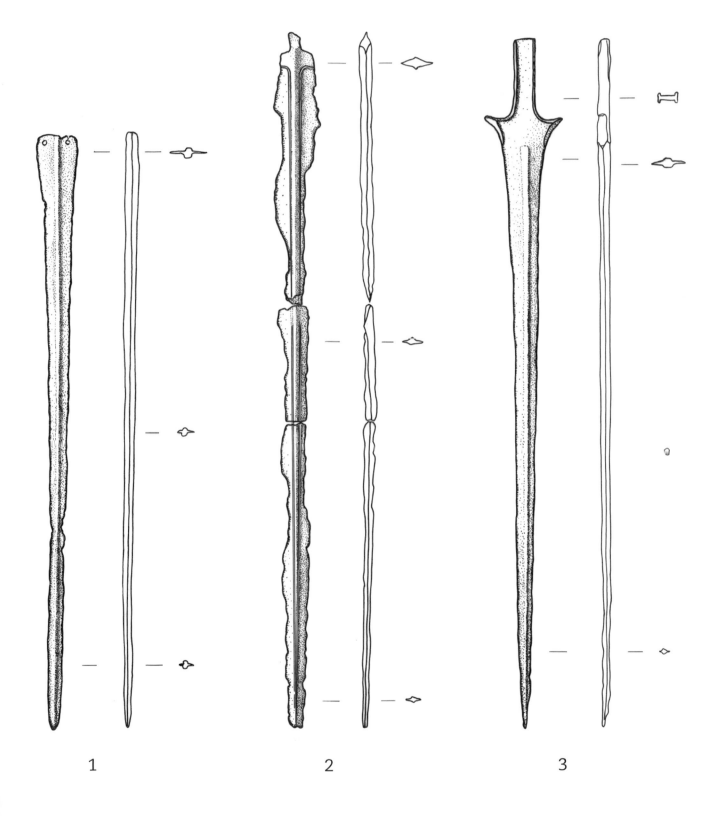

1   2   3

Plate II

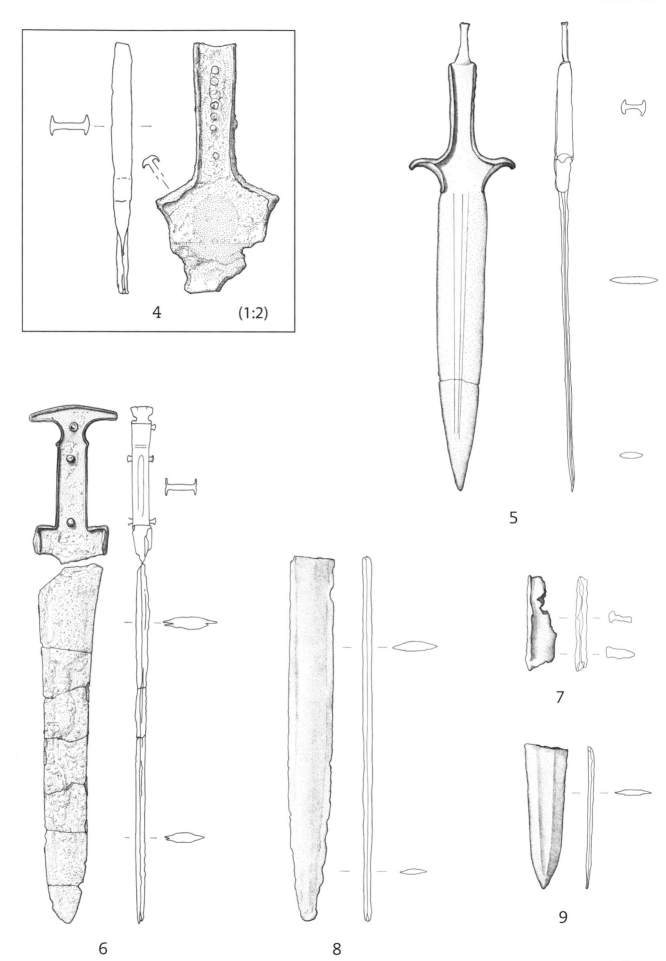

4 (1:2)

5

6

7

8

9

1:3

Plate III

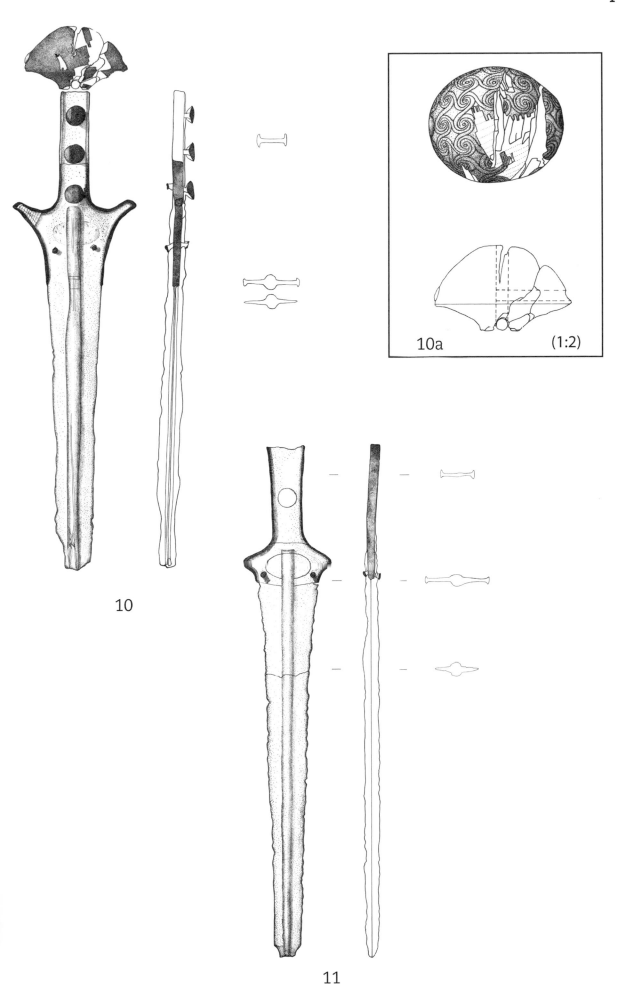

10a   (1:2)

10

11

1:3

Plate IV

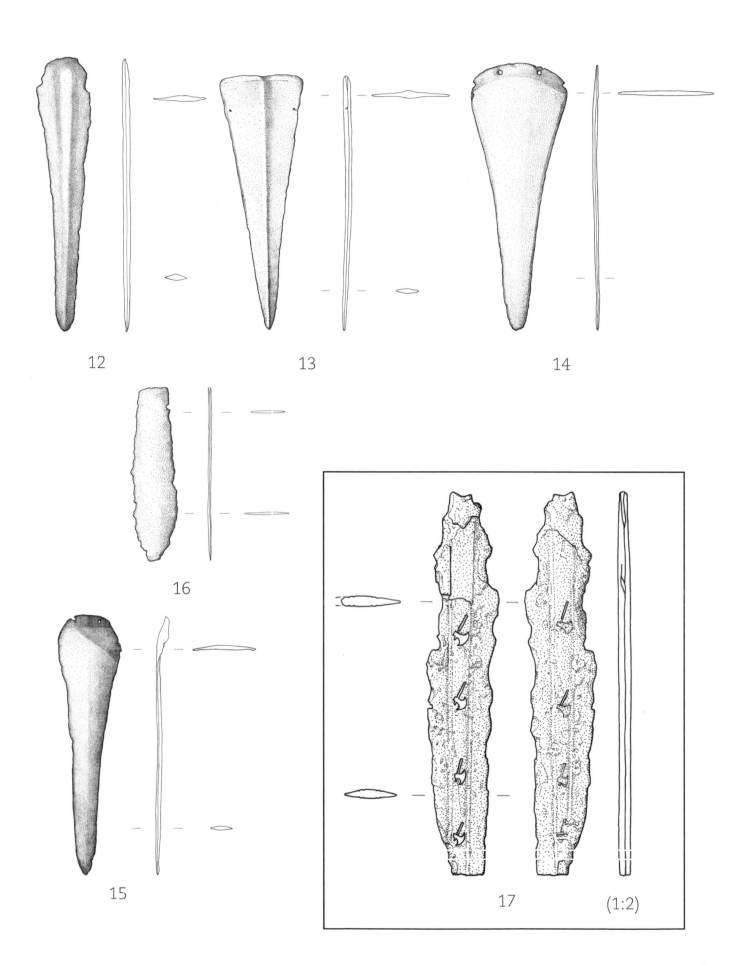

12

13

14

16

15

17

(1:2)

1:3

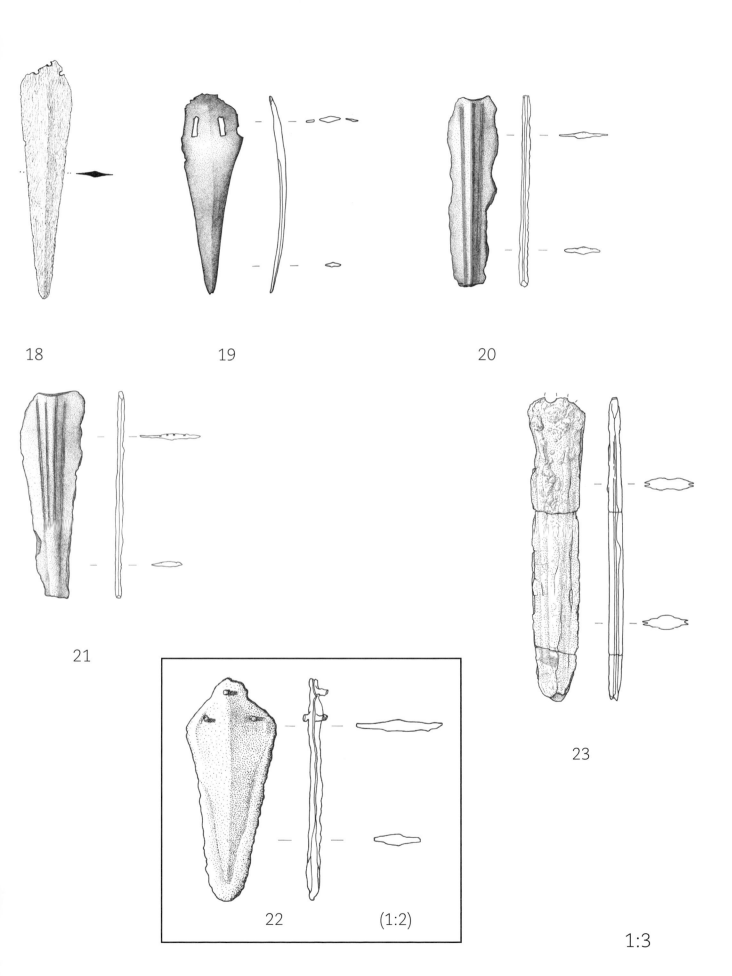

Plate V

1:3

18

19

20

21

22 (1:2)

23

Plate VI

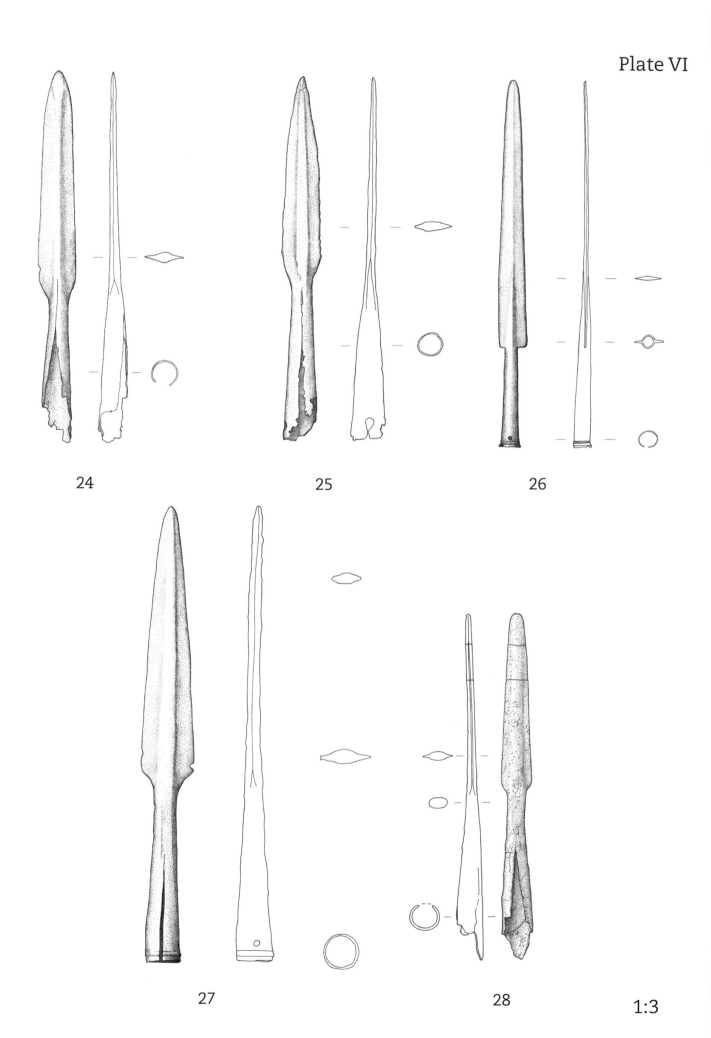

24

25

26

27

28

1:3

Plate VII

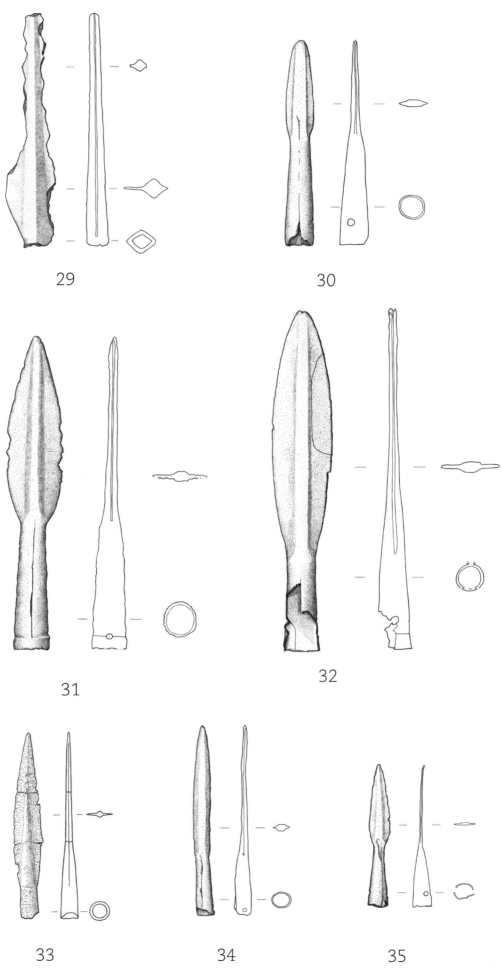

29

30

31

32

33

34

35

1:3

Plate VIII

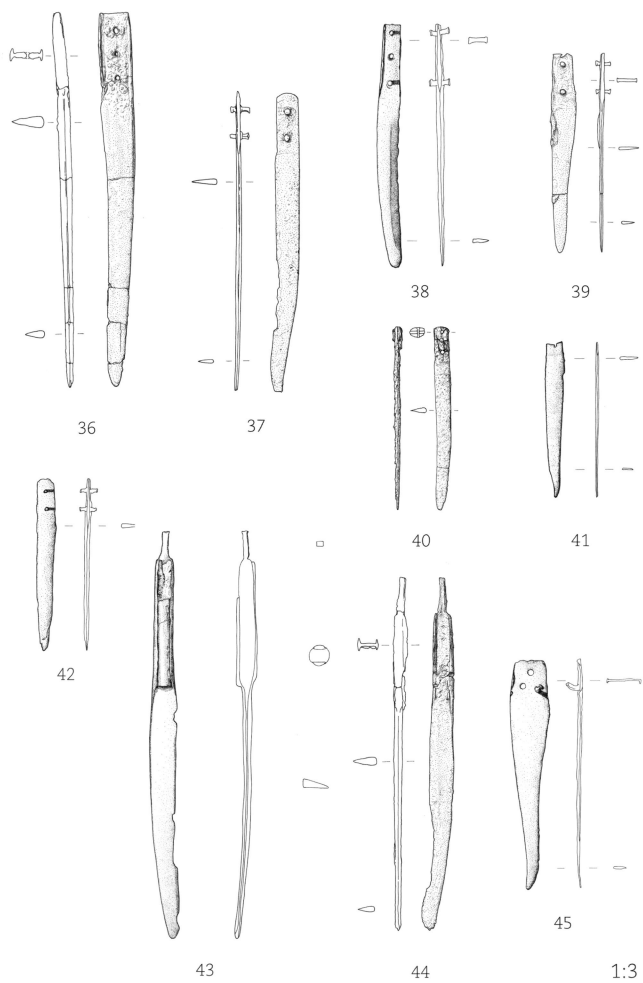

36

37

38

39

40

41

42

43

44

45

1:3

Plate IX

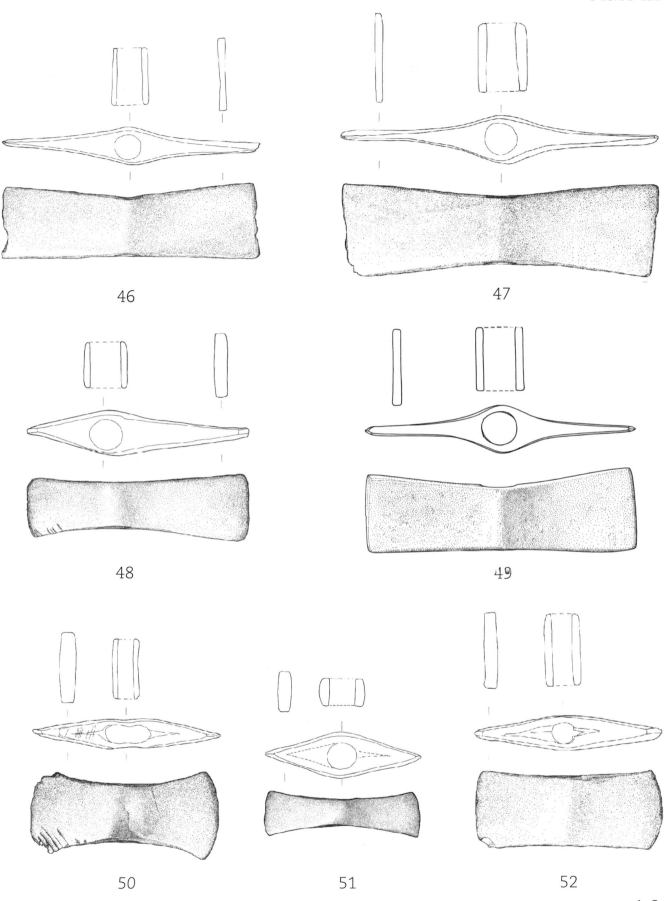

46

47

48

49

50

51

52

1:3

Plate X

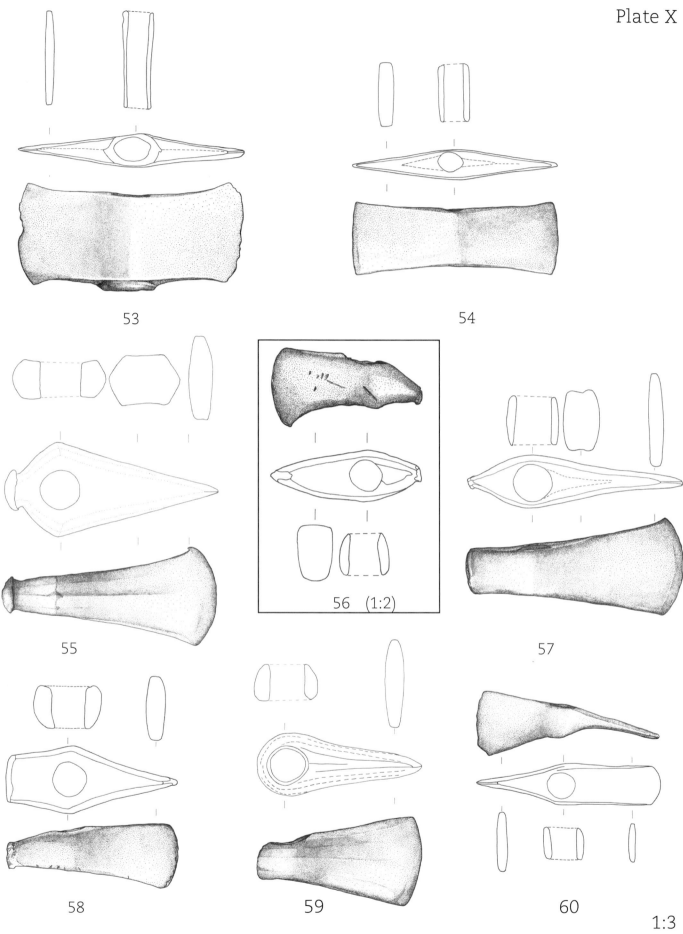

53

54

55

56 (1:2)

57

58

59

60

1:3

Plate XI

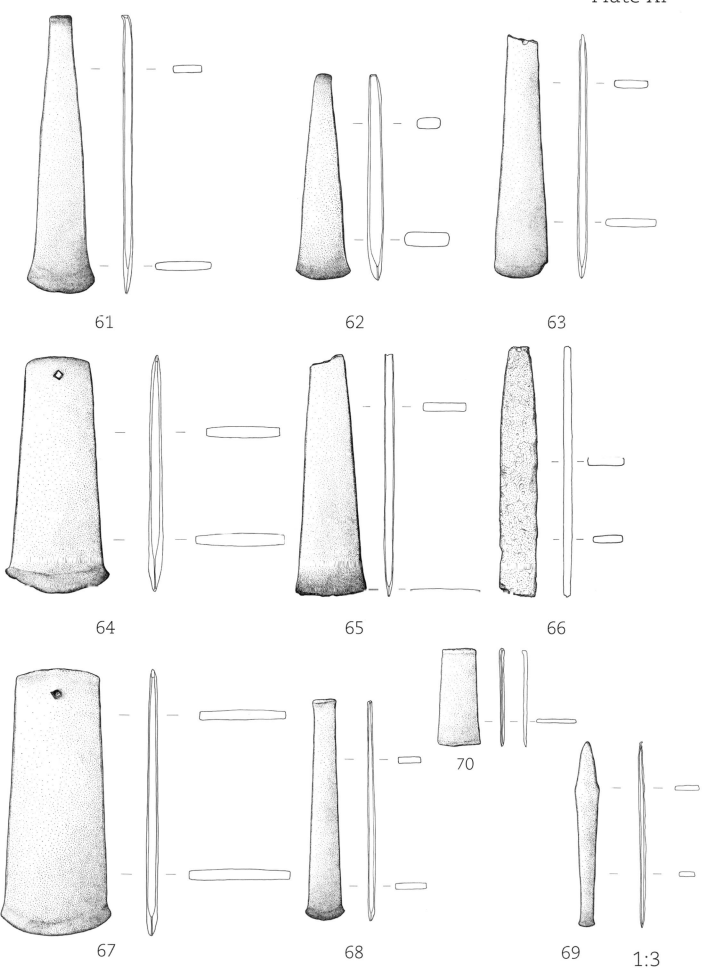

61

62

63

64

65

66

67

68

69

70

1:3

Plate XII

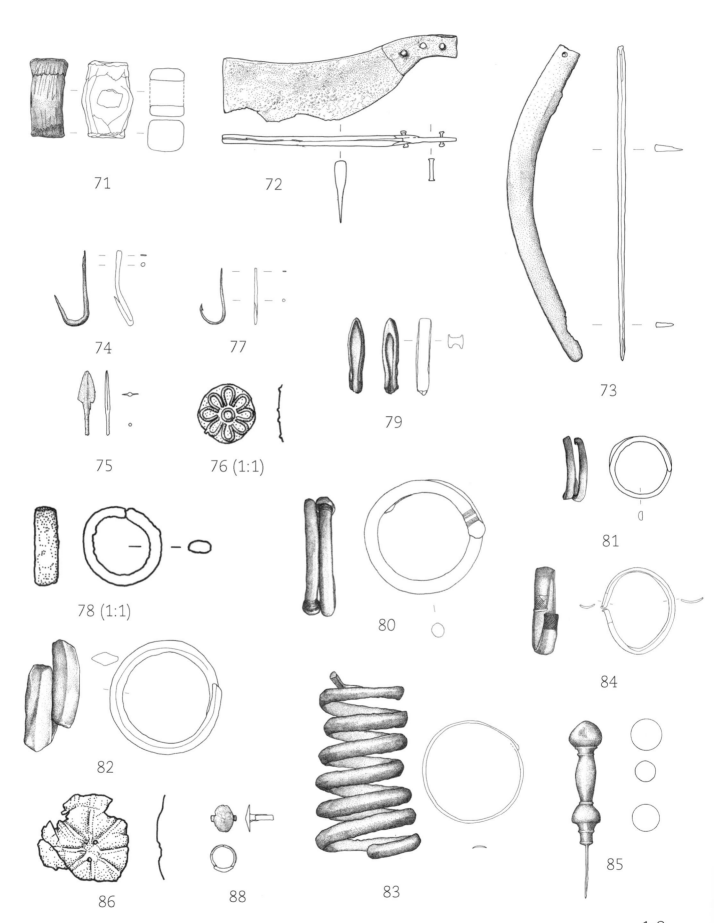

71

72

73

74

77

79

75

76 (1:1)

81

78 (1:1)

80

84

82

85

86

88

83

1:3

Plate XIII

TROY

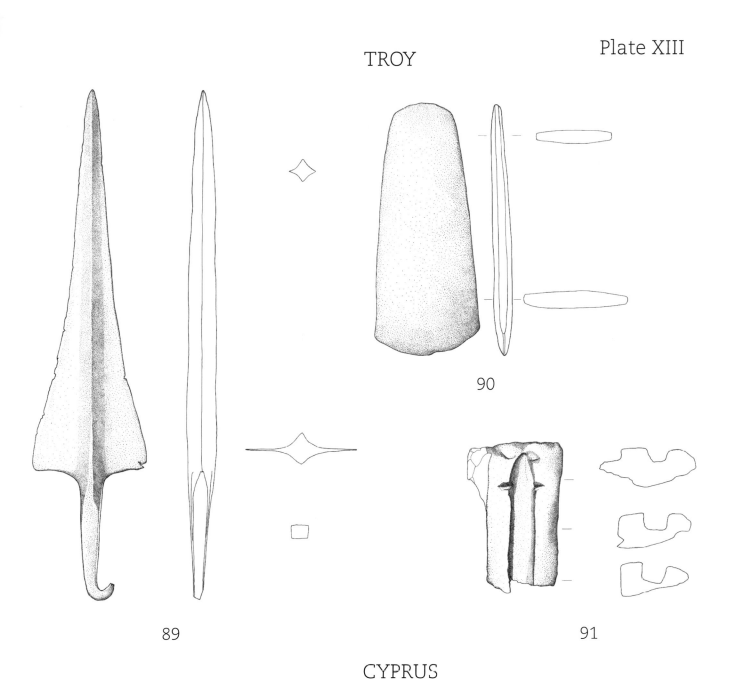

90

89

91

CYPRUS

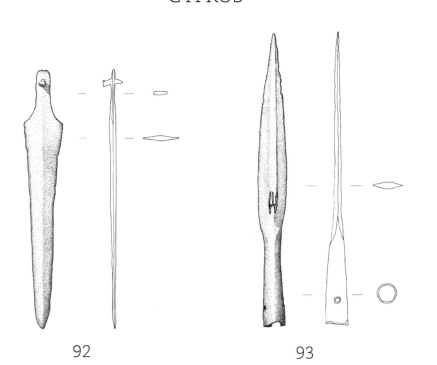

92

93

1:3

Plate XIV

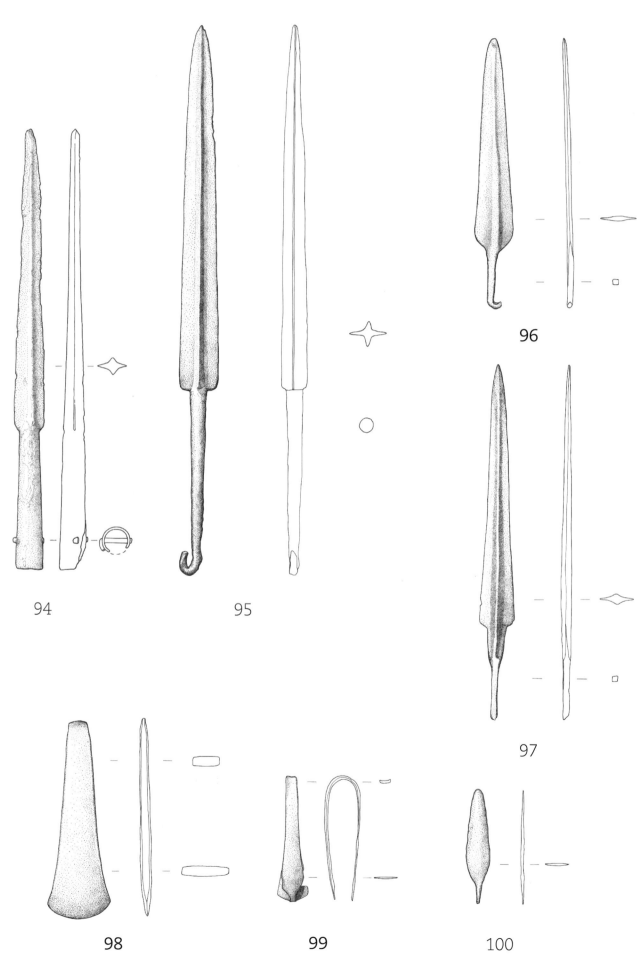

94

95

96

97

98

99

100

1:3

(CYPRUS CONTINUED)

Plate XV

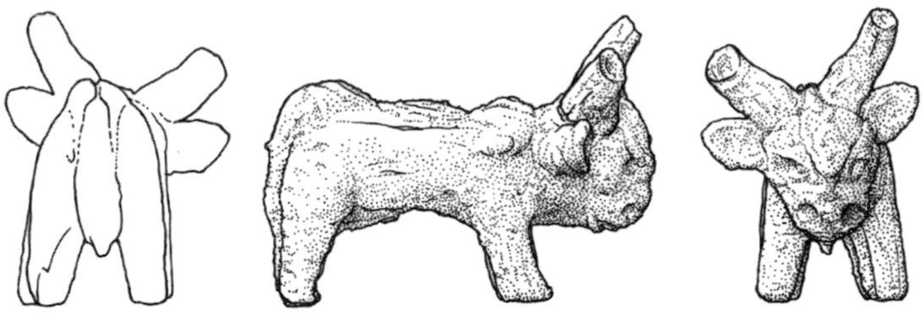

101 (1:2)

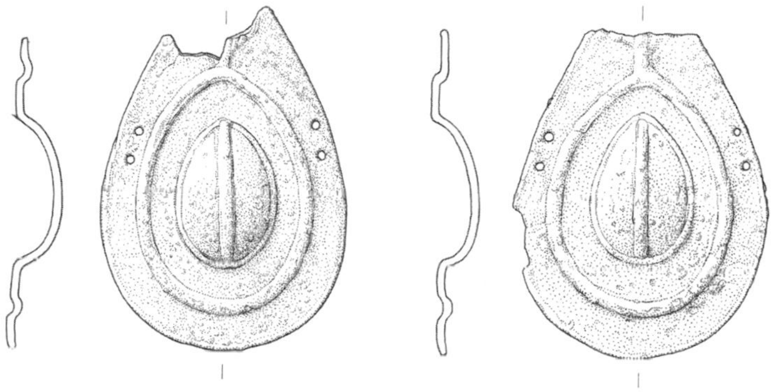

102

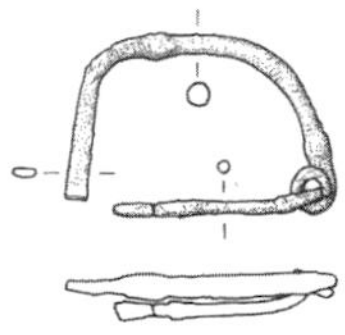

103

THE NEAR EAST

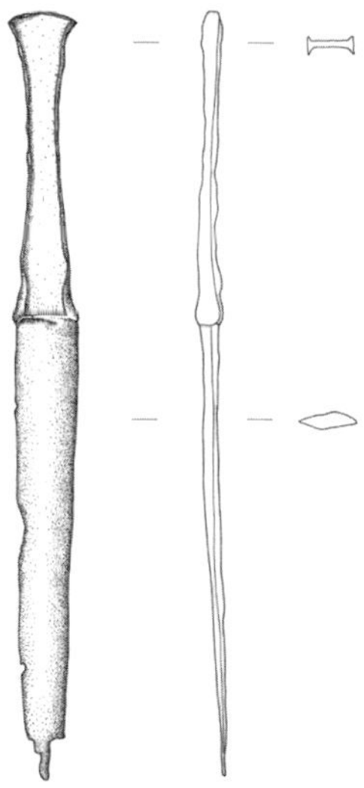

105

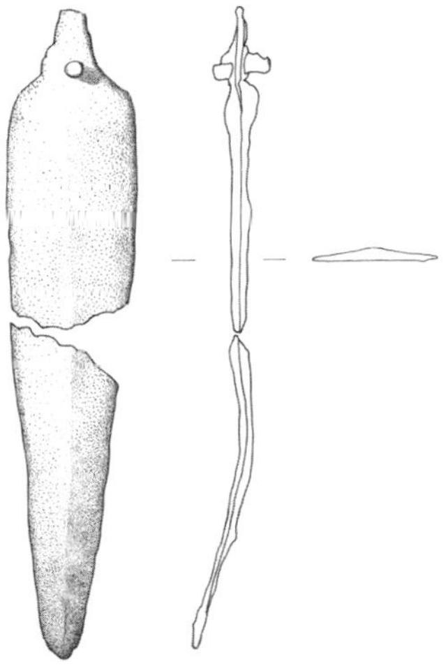

107

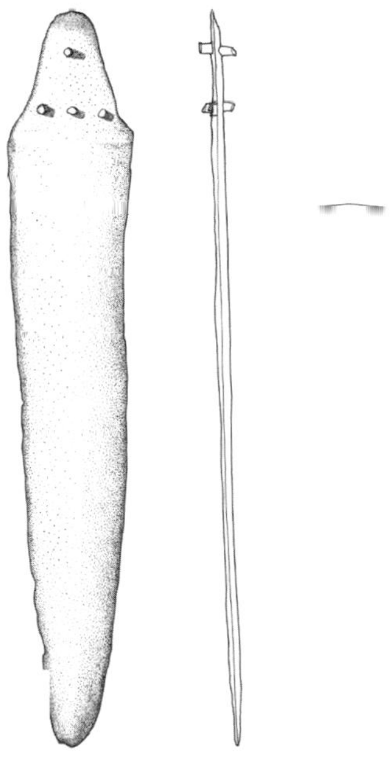

106

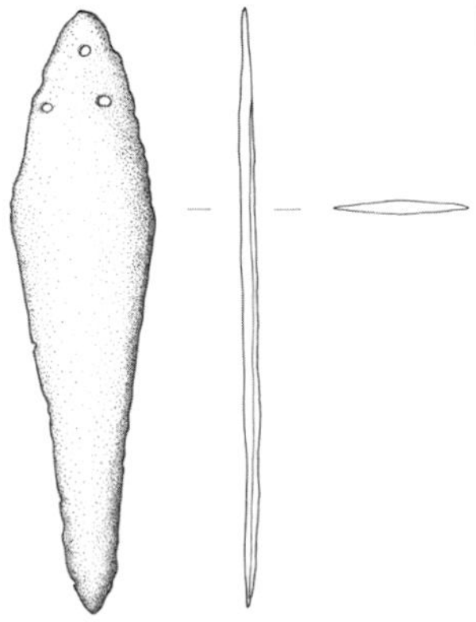

108

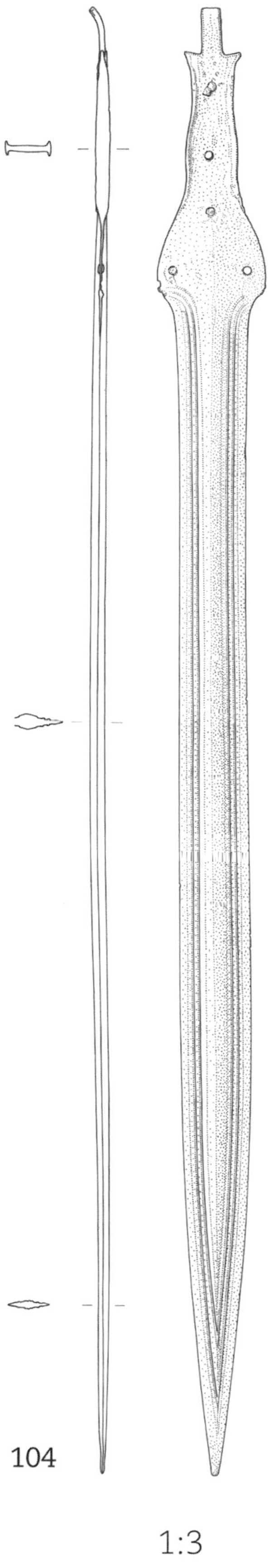

104

1:3

Plate XVI

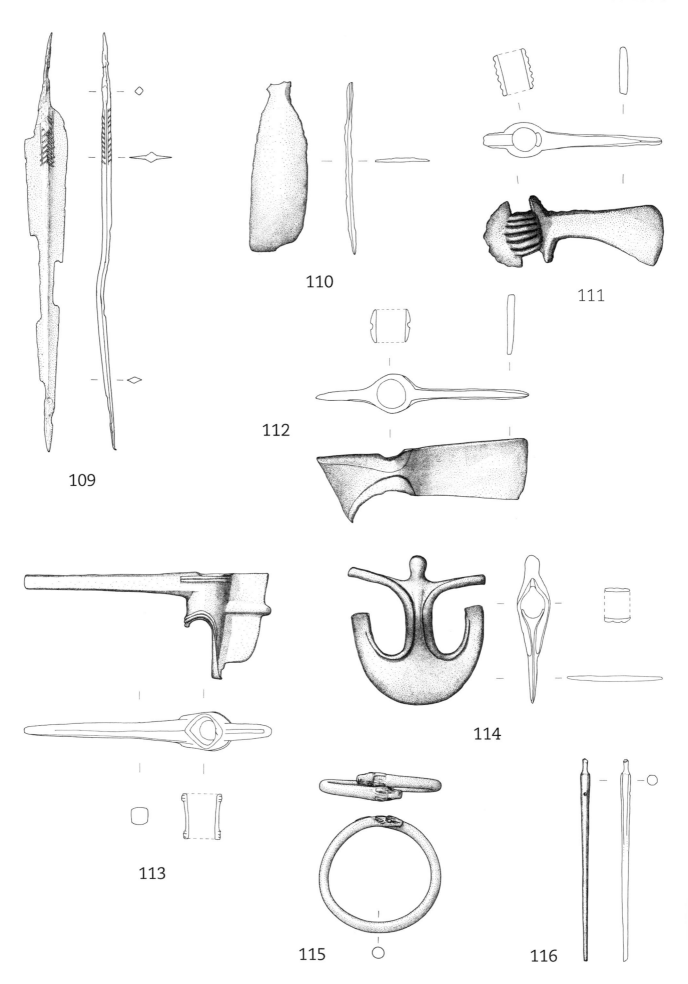

109

110

111

112

113

114

115

116

1:3

Plate XVII

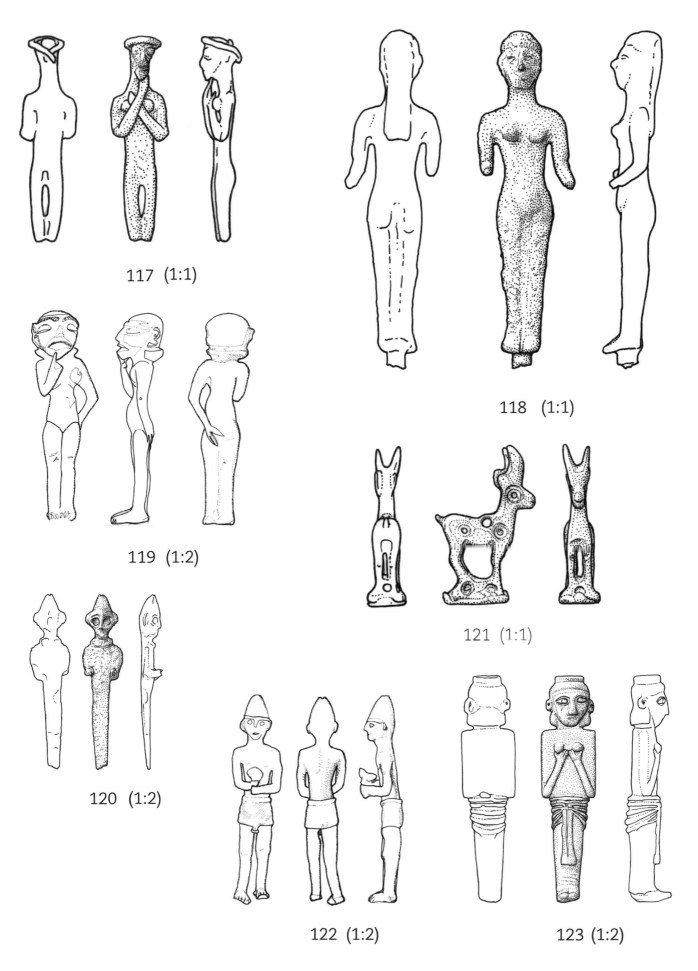

117 (1:1)

118 (1:1)

119 (1:2)

121 (1:1)

120 (1:2)

122 (1:2)

123 (1:2)

1:1 and 1:2

Plate XVIII

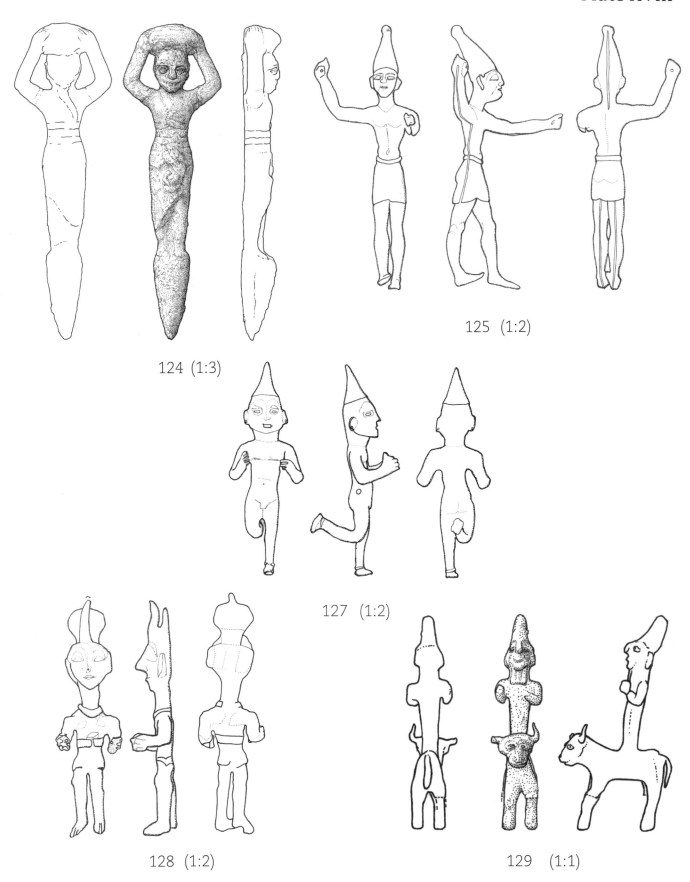

124 (1:3)

125 (1:2)

127 (1:2)

128 (1:2)

129 (1:1)

Various dimensions

Plate XIX

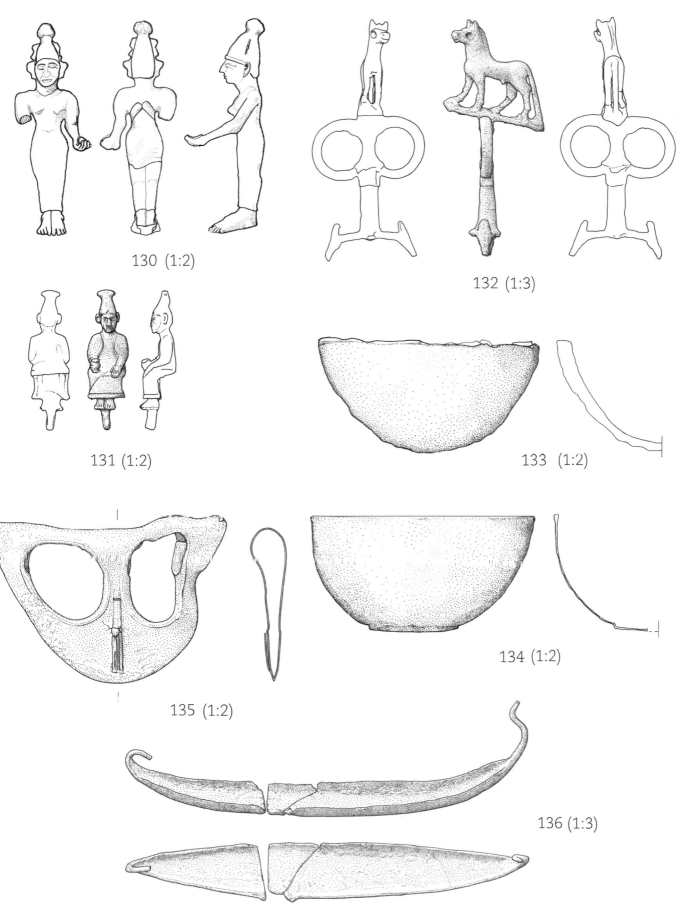

130 (1:2)

132 (1:3)

131 (1:2)

133 (1:2)

135 (1:2)

134 (1:2)

136 (1:3)

Various dimensions

Plate XX

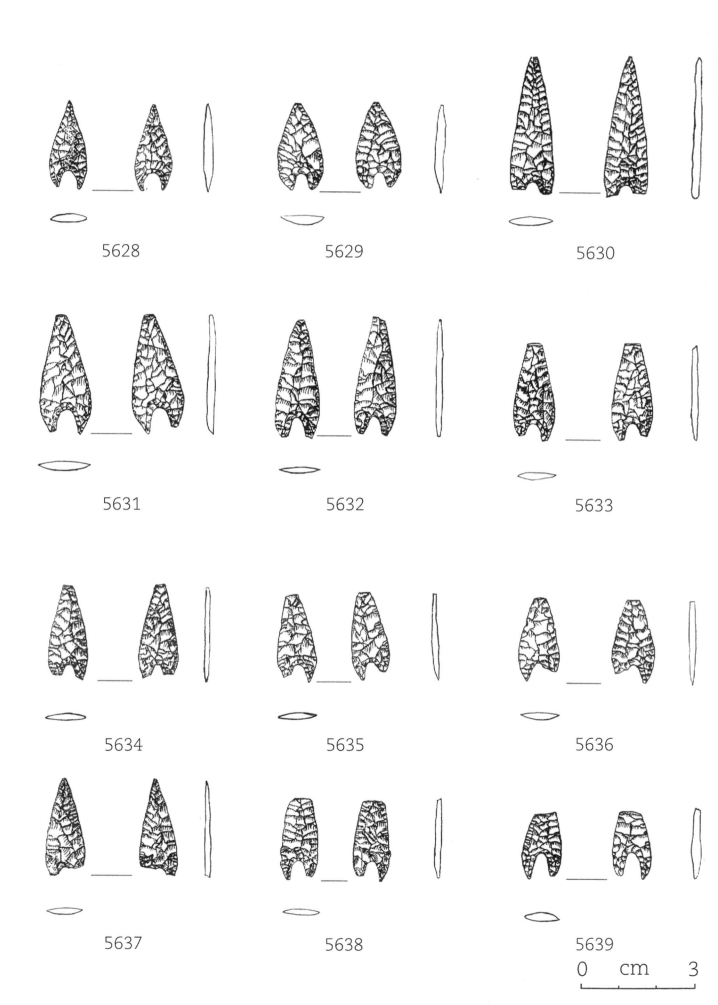

5628

5629

5630

5631

5632

5633

5634

5635

5636

5637

5638

5639

0　cm　3

Plate XXI

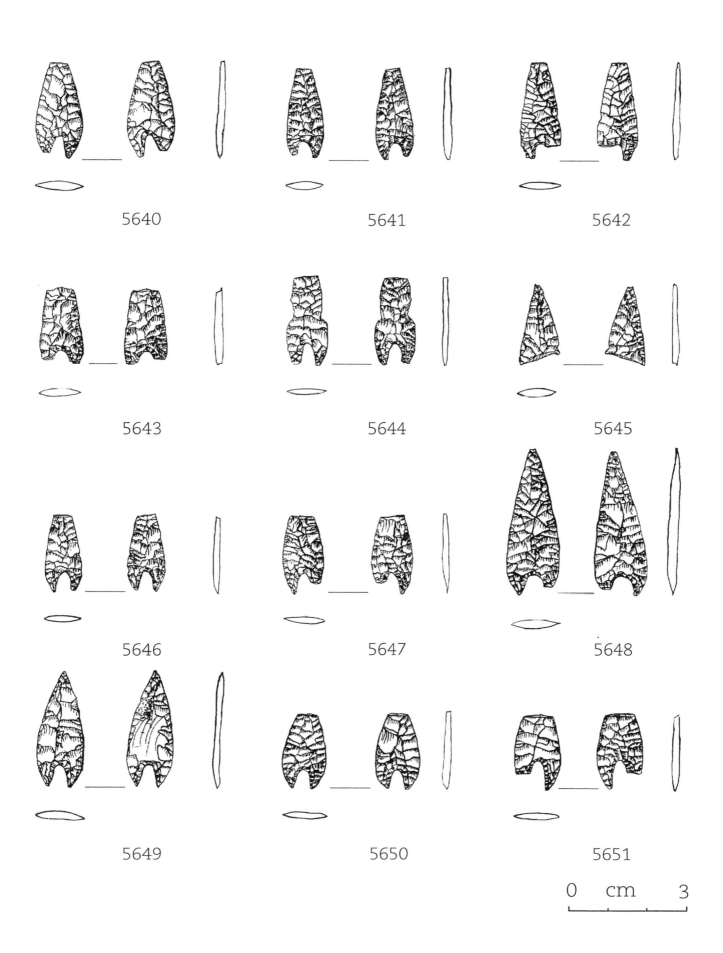

5640

5641

5642

5643

5644

5645

5646

5647

5648

5649

5650

5651

0   cm   3

Plate XXII

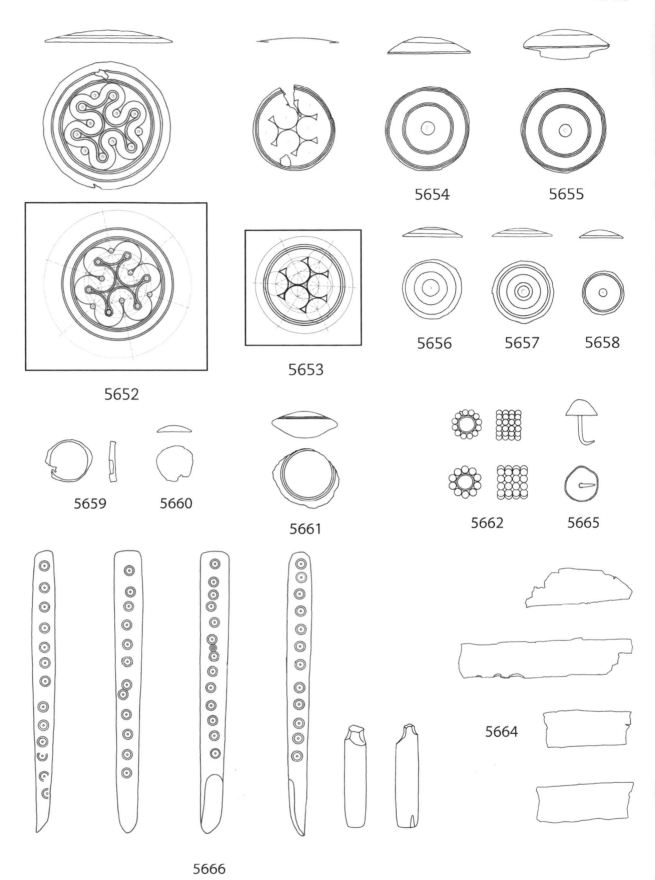

5654

5655

5652

5653

5656

5657

5658

5659

5660

5661

5662

5665

5664

5666

1:1